choose JOY

A Survivor's Guide for Hope

Amy
Love Nancy

Nancy Nance

Editor: Judi Fennell
Photographer:
Cover Image: Adobe Stock
Cover Design: Angie Ayalya
Interior Design: Marigold2k
Publisher: Spotlight Publishing House™
https://SpotlightPublishingHouse.com

Endorsements

I loved every minute of reading *Choose Joy: A Survivor's Guide for Hope.*

It drew me in, and I couldn't put it down.

This is a book for anyone who has EVER struggled with grief or the feeling of not being enough.

Thank you Nancy for sharing your journey of tragedy to triumph so eloquently with all of us.

It is wonderful how you walked us though the steps you used to turn the Lights on after living in the darkness for so many years.

Reading your different life experiences showed me how, as you said, Forgiveness does not change the past. Forgiveness enlarges the future.

I am so grateful for how your words have assisted me to now allow my angels to guide me more to do what brings me joy.
—**Daphne McDonagh,** Healing Energy Coach, Rehabilitation and Wellness Specialist, 2x International Bestselling Author
www.daphneshealinghands.com

"This is a story of self-transformation, the survivor's guide of story that we wish was never told, but the truth to the power within. This is a story that's original to none of us, but only original to us because of a different cast, different location, an original as to the action we take, long after we have wiped tear after tear from the sides of our face.

This is a story about loving you right where you are right now and owning your truth and dealing with life head on, because moments matter.

The words are magical, her story is her truth, I have learned that you don't build trust by offering help, we build trust by asking for help, this book is the"ask."

This is a must-read book, because within each page there are words which tell a story that you are holding within. So, to grow you must make some mistakes, to be confident, you must face your fears and anxieties, to live you most forgive yourself, and hold you accountable. To learn, you have to let go of some stuff, to exist you have to show up as more and give back just because, and to understand inner strength, you have to understand the power of your words and share and tell this story. I hope you *Choose Joy*."

—**Kevin McLemore,** Award winning author, Fitness Professional, Host of two Podcasts "Talking with Kevin and Son," and" Motivation Sundays with Kevin and Friends", Artist, AKA "The Mindset Messenger."

"Choose Joy: A Survivor's Guide for Hope is more than a book— it's a roadmap to personal transformation. Nancy's courage and fierce determination shine through every page as she lays out the tools you need to shift from surviving to thriving.

If life's hardships have left you feeling stuck or overwhelmed, this book will remind you of your inner strength. Nancy doesn't just share her story; she hands you the blueprint for breaking free from the grip of trauma and embracing a future full of purpose and joy.

With her heartfelt wisdom and actionable strategies, you will feel empowered to release the past, take charge of your healing, and rediscover your true potential. This is not just a read—it's your invitation to a whole new way of living."
—**Christopher Rausch**, Coach | Speaker | Host | Author
www.ChristopherRausch.com

"We have all seen 'those women'. The women that struggle to hold their families together, to be a positive influence for their children despite what is happening behind closed doors. Nancy's journey through her life is tragic and inspiring at the same time. Her deep desire to want more but didn't have any idea on how to get it, until one day things changed. Her life had finally hit the low point, rock bottom and now there was no way but up. Picking herself up by her boot straps, she clawed her way to freedom. Freedom from her past and freedom from all the terrible events that haunted her. Nancy's story is one of resilience and she shows you how a person determined to success in life will."
—**Brenda Hammon,** www.brendahammon-author

"As the publisher of Ignite Joy, I intimately understand the transformative power that joy can bring to one's life. I also recognize the unwavering dedication and deep sense of self-worth required to reach that blessed state. Nancy has courageously walked this path and discovered the joy in life that she truly deserves. Her story exemplifies the hard work and perseverance it takes to move beyond challenging circumstances and decide, against all odds, to choose joy. Nancy not only embraces joy for herself but also becomes a beacon of light, reflecting that joy for others. Her journey is a testament to the human spirit's resilience and the profound impact of choosing positivity in the face of adversity. 'Choose

Joy' is an inspiring guide for anyone seeking to transform their life through the power of joyful living."
—**Lady JB Owen,** ROC, Global Speaker, Philanthropist, Humanitarian, and Founder of Ignite Publishing and Ignite Humanity

"Reading *Choose Joy*, Nancy's authentic journey evokes real and raw emotions—despair, anger, devastating grief, and ultimately healing and joy—making the title a mantra for those facing life-changing events."
—**Karin Lisa** - Inspiritual Intuitive

"I had the honour of getting to know Nancy and it is an honor to feature such a powerful connection. Ever since I came across her, I had to connect with her, and she has taught me how to get connected to myself on a spiritual level. In this book I can believe that many more will be connected to their spiritual self."
—**Adam Duval**, The Mental Health Warriors Podcast

"Nancy Nance's story is a raw, honest, and uncensored account of her journey to forgiveness and joy. Nancy shares her truth and delves into the darkness of the soul, depicting the human experience.

By making her story relatable, she repeatedly chooses joy, inspiring others to do the same. *"The more I changed my mindset, the less I resonated with the victim mentality."* Ultimately, she chooses joy even in the most impossible circumstances."
—**Jo Dibblee**, Humanitarian, Author, Founder

"A direct and rich memoir written with authenticity, Nancy Nance courageously shares her story of grief, loss, strength, faith, and trust. For anyone who has ever experienced loss or had to let go, this is the book to read!

Thank you for sharing your story with us and for reminding us how to keep the joy going, how to continue believing, even in the midst of letting go unprepared."
—**S. Essnaashari**, DO (EU), DOMP, HOM

A Survivor's Guide for Hope

Nancy Nance

SPOTLIGHT
PUBLISHING HOUSE
Goodyear, Arizona

Contents

Author's Note

This memoir has been pieced together with the help of journals. Great care has been taken to tell my truths. This is my story and how I remember it.

Introduction

Choose Joy is a survival guide for anyone who has been or will ever feel broken by life. It is a handbook for hope designed to help you find peace. Learning to navigate through the places you travel in life is easier with a friendly guide, easy to understand map and success strategy. A guide gives you something to hold onto as you wait for the pain to end. A map shows you that there are many places to travel. A strategy offers you action steps to take to help you achieve success.

My hope is to inspire you to believe in your ability to forgive, embrace peace and create a life that shares the gift of you. The journey of forgiveness is different for everyone. Pain and peace are valuable pinpoints on the map of life that can lead to forgiveness. I have walked through my own personal hell and clawed my way up through the depths of despair. The strategies I used have helped me journey to happiness successfully. My journey could have killed me, and I could have killed. I am grateful I decided to *Choose Joy*.

This book is a relatable journey of traveling through hell to a place of peace, compassion and forgiveness that will reveal that happiness is an option. Living your best life is still possible. The rest of your life can be the best of your life; all things are possible. There is more to your life than what you may be currently settling for. You deserve the best. I want to inspire you to be the person that someone looks at and says, "Because of you, I didn't give up."

Being a human isn't always easy. Difficult challenges and every-day-stressors create times when it could seem easier to just give up. This book is for the champion in you who refuses to surrender.

Faith is a cornerstone for peace. Life without faith is no life at all. Believe that better is coming. Trust that your breakthrough is near. It is essential to trust that this is your year to win. This is your season for growth. Now is your time to heal.

I began writing this book for my friends, family and clients. I continued and discovered that *Choose Joy* was written for every daughter, mother, son or father who has been touched by loss. Life and death have meaning and purpose. Life gives us hope, death can be painful, and grief teaches us to value life.

I wrote this book to encourage you to travel through the hell of your life and believe that peace is possible. Finding peaceful moments as you navigate the challenges and obstacles in your life will allow you to stay the course when you want to quit.

Choose Joy is for the dreamer in you that is willing to risk leaving the comfort zone to create an exciting, passionate life filled with love, laughter and happily ever after. I wrote this book to *inspire* you to believe you can be the champion in your own healing journey. I believe that your dream is worth pursuing and your happiness matters. Your life and what you share with the world is a gift.

Writing a book about joy and survival was a journey that allowed me to remember how valuable hope is. More money can be earned, yet more days cannot be bought. Hope offers another day and the opportunity to create. I am intrigued by how human beings are busy doing while often missing the freedom of being. How much does the cost of fighting to survive impact overall happiness? Do the people we meet in life have the power to change our lives? When does the desire to increase joy in life become more powerful than the pain we suffer? My wish is that this book gives you, dear reader, a few answers to these questions.

My story is as unique as the sunrise I see every morning. The ever-changing beauty is one of the many ways that hope purposefully rises each day. I am a soul with a purpose. As a human, I have learned to be more content as I strive to live a gentle life with peaceful compassion. Gratitude helps me see abundance in my life and celebrate every day.

Choose Joy Breakthrough Coaching allows me to encourage, nudge, support and empower many. I am blessed to provide guidance towards healing and wellness. The life we create through words, wonder, experiences, challenges, choices, success and defeat are our legacy. Healing and wholeness have helped me find a deep lasting joy that supports my life during trauma, struggle, suffering and pain. I understand the importance of congruency between my thoughts, actions, beliefs, and manifestations. I have learned how to transform obstacles into opportunities because I see the choices within the challenges. The relationship that exists between what I focus on and what I receive is shown by the happiness I radiate.

Kindness is a gift we give to ourselves and others. Hope is a blessing that allows us to trust that pain can end. Sharing joy through kindness and hope is my mission, passion and purpose.

Story offers the opportunity to experience the life of another. One word joined with another builds a story and ultimately a guidebook that offers you the chance to create a life with more joy. I am excited for you to join me on this journey.

My intention is to share the tangled threads and beautiful tapestry of my life. I have experienced the beauty of love and seen the unfolding of death. I break through boundaries and understand transformational effects. I am a rebel with a cause and a humble, peaceful warrior. I know that battling through life with an axe seeking vengeful justice does not align with my joyful journey. Peace is power and love is beauty. Butterflies, rainbows, sunsets and laughter are reminders that shine the light of love and hope for another tomorrow.

My wish for you is that you wake to another day willing to embrace the opportunity to change and live a more purposeful existence. I offer help to others who have gone through similar situations. Together we learn from the mistakes we have made.

View my special message by scanning the code below OR go to: https://qrco.de/ChooseJoyIntroduction

Prologue

I woke up one August morning in 2011 to a different day. This was the day I would choose to live my life without my forever friend and joy. August 26, 2011, the day my daughter, Emily Joy, died and her brother, my son Jarett survived changed my life forever. The love that held our family together shattered when a boat swerved to miss one Sea-doo and crashed into another which carried my son and his sister.

My daughter died instantly. My son survived. Our lives changed. Emily's death was the catalyst for the breakdown of my marriage. I looked for a way to find closure to an accident that was deemed no fault. I fell out of love with my husband and into faith for a better tomorrow. The dysfunction of a twenty-five-year marriage crumbled within a year when my husband left our life for another woman. I learned to forgive myself for staying in a marriage that was damaged by a man who chose drugs and other women. I searched for a way to forgive the billionaire boat driver who never sought to connect with my son to assure him Emily's death wasn't his fault. I dredged up every bit of pain, survived and recovered. I chose to heal and live a life with joy.

Choosing to live without joy would have been like choosing to enjoy living without my other children. There was absolutely no doubt that there was any other choice. Jarett, my first-born son, was my breath and my heartbeat. Chance, my second-born son, was my sunrise and my smile. Even though my heart was broken, I walked forward toward healing knowing my sons needed me as much as I needed them.

Walking forward away from my painful past toward healing and a life of joy was a choice I made to overcome the agony of parenting without a child. Grief and loss are life lessons we all endure. No one can escape this world without experiencing the sorrow of loss. The words I use to express my mortal understanding of this incredible life of mine are a gift that help me heal. I offer these words as my gift to you. Thank you for opening this book and your eyes, to read the words on this page.

When the going got tough—and it often did—I trusted that I would be guided. I believed that I would be steered to a forever friend to help make my life worth living. Before Emily died, I had a faith in a power greater than me. I believed in angels and trusted their loving guidance. Even though I struggled with my faith in God and Jesus, I prayed to Emily. I trusted that she would help me stay willing to take a forever friend's hand, follow their footsteps, and walk forward together. I longed for loving support to help me through the tough times. I ached to create more memories with family and friends. I imagined listening to the beauty of Christmas, savoring the laughter, enjoying happiness, and opening presents together.

Life, with Emily's assistance, steered me to a forever friend and more. I learned that this game of life is much more fun with sparkles. The people you meet are the sparkles that make the game possible. They spark ideas and adventures. Be grateful for each one of them. Friends create memories with you, support you when life is challenging, encourage you when you want to quit and celebrate with you when you win. Be a sparkle for your friends too. Give the world the gift of you. You have the power to create your day. Each obstacle and opportunity will guide you through today toward tomorrow.

Be grateful for the privilege and pleasure of today. Look for the pleasures in life. Hear the laughter, taste the sweet lemon drops and gooey gumdrops, touch the tears, smell the rain, and trust together. You are not alone. Your ride or die partner, your forever friend is out in this world waiting to meet you. There are many friends waiting for the privilege of connecting with you. You matter to them even if you haven't met them yet. You have the potential to make a difference in the life of another.

Take the day you have and create something. Creation is life. Bake a cake, blow bubbles with a child, help your neighbor or pick up the phone and create a conversation. Creating helps the heart feel alive. Create for ten days and then ten more. Being creative and practicing creativity will help you thrive. Add ten more days of creating until you reach 40, 50, 60, 70, 80, 90 days. Share your creations with your friends and family. See the happiness you bring them. Creating is a spark that ignites the imagination of another. Become the sparkles you want to see in the world.

Tell someone how much they matter. Encouragement is a powerful offering of love. As a mother, I have learned the value of encouraging my children daily. I see the difference that encouragement makes when I look into the eyes of my grandchildren as I praise them for the beauty they create in this world. Telling someone they matter and cheering them on with encouragement improves your wellbeing and theirs. I encourage you to make a new friend, smile at a stranger, pet a puppy. Plant a seed, open a door, take a walk, see the world. Today is a gift. Yesterday is the history you created.

My intention is to guide you to a life with much more joy. More joy is a life filled with purpose that lights you up and enriches the lives of those around you. Forgiveness is a pinpoint on this journey. Reading this book will help you identify possible blocks and obstacles in your life. Analyzing your own obstacles and challenges will allow you to explore what in life has been stopping you from accessing joy. What would more joy in your life look like? How valuable is it to you? Reading *Choose Joy: A*

Survivor's Guide for Hope is your opportunity to identify blocks, obstacles, challenges and then learn how to choose to create openings and opportunities to share the gift of you and create much more joy.

View my special message by scanning the code below
OR go to: https://qrco.de/ChooseJoy_Prologue

Chapter 1

Never Ever Again

I lived in a land of *Never Ever Again*, trapped between the rivers of *Maybe Next Time It'll Be Better* and *It Really Isn't That Bad.* Living in denial was an ugly existence because I believed that my captor held the key to my freedom. I was conditioned by my husband Terry's abuse. The battery left deep scars in my mind. I hid bruises with long sleeves and scarves around my neck. Black circles from tear-filled nights were concealed behind dollar-store sunglasses. My throat ached from yelling into my pillow. I did not want to wake or worry the children. No one heard my cry, so I stayed.

I quietly remained in *Never Ever Again* land, plotting for my escape while watching from behind the bars of my castle cage. The castle cage was within our home that sat on a hill in Sturgeon Valley north of St. Albert in the prairie province of Alberta. We lived there since 2001 the year I carried my daughter Emily in my womb. I persisted for one more Christmas in our eight-thousand-square-foot castle. I was hopeful the new year would bring a solution to my financial mess.

I was carrying a heavy burden. On the outside I appeared to be a happy wife with a well-put-together family. The weight was a massive debt load and a thousand broken promises. I was obligated to pay the mortgage which was an expense we could barely afford. Groceries were removed from the till when the checking account was once again overdrawn. The cashier huffed and puffed as I chose what to remove. I was embarrassed and ashamed. Not all the bills could be paid and each month I decided what needed to be prioritized. We could not afford the

1

five-piece leather sectional that was on hold at the furniture store. I became tired of giving excuses to the salesman who called asking when we would be finalizing the sales order, so I stopped answering his calls. The expenses were increasingly more than the income.

I worked daily at the office of our construction company. I managed our home and kept our five children happy. Eight-thousand-square feet was costing me and my children millions of dollars and broken promises. The line of credit against our estate home investment was overdrawn. Money was owed to multiple debtors. If my husband were to die, he would die with a massive debt. The estate, my children and I, would be held liable for all money owing. I had to stay until I was able to change the financial deficit into financial abundance. We were paying a heavy cost to appear to be a happy well-put-together family.

I was willing to spend another Christmas in our estate home on Manor View Crescent hopeful that my children would share the beauty of family, laughter, happiness, and opening presents. I planned for a joyful celebration and invited twenty-one guests, mostly family, for dinner.

Christmas morning looked perfect, with snow glistening on the trees that surrounded our yard. A beautiful eight-foot-tall pine tree stood in the living room. Our massive living room held our second hand six-chair dining room set and two plastic folding tables with fifteen collapsible chairs. Underneath the tree were gifts for our five children. Emily, our daughter, was adorable in her red and white velvet dress. She was two years old and did not realize that daddy was absent. My four sons, Spencer, Joshua, Jarett and Chance were accustomed to Terry's benders and chronic absences. Clint, Terry's ex-brother-in-law from his previous marriage to Spencer's mother, lived with us. He kindly offered to make breakfast while I drove to pick up Alice my mom. He assured me that he would wake all the boys and that they would be dressed and fed before we returned.

During the drive Mom questioned me about Terry's absence and my behavior. I called her before I left and told her that he had chosen to not be with his family. He chose to abandon us for a crack cocaine bender. Mom wondered why he used crack cocaine. More than ten years of continued crack use and an abundance of absences led her to pose a valid question: "Maybe if he just used cocaine instead of crack, he would be with us." I explained that he started with cocaine years ago and his habit escalated to crack. I elaborated and explained that crack is a concentrate that is smoked. Crack cocaine gets its name from the crackling sound the rock makes when it's heated.

I knew that Mom was asking because she truly cared and wanted to help find a solution. As tears pooled in my eyes, I explained that powdered cocaine damages the nose, and that crack cocaine damages the lungs. I took a deep breath, cleared my throat and spoke the truth, "Mom, Terry is an addict. He is the one that must choose to get help." Mom reached out and touched my hand. Her words of reassurance, "I understand" allowed me to move forward to the rest of Christmas day. Unburdening my heart felt wonderful.

For years, it had been easier to lie to Mom about Terry's addictions than burden her with the truth. Admitting that I had married an alcoholic, drug and gambling addict didn't fit into the, "What's new? How are the kids? Is Terry at home or at work?" mother and daughter dialogue of our relationship. I often told her Terry was working out of town until the gap between his benders became too small. Terry would be home for just five days then would go missing for three.

Terry's mother Heather and his sister Leslie were more persistent when Terry didn't answer his phone. His one, two, three-day benders created phone calls to me. The series of questions: "Is he home yet? What happened to make him want to go out? Did you two have a fight?" were a challenge to answer without further upsetting the kids. Phone messages were left and answered later when I was alone. Eventually, I stopped answering calls from his mother and sister and would text when he arrived home. It was less painful to sit in the darkness of my home than share my heart with his family. Too many birthday parties, sports events, and Sunday gatherings with questions about a missing Terry had left me feeling drained and exhausted. I was tired of discussions with his family about what would we do to solve the problem of his absence.

Christmas was my focus and creating the best possible day was my mission. Even though Terry was absent and the questions from family would probably begin again, I trusted that I would be able to enjoy the moments of joy. When Mom and I opened the door, all the boys were awake. It was time to open the presents.

I enjoyed giving gifts and loved the special hand-made gifts that my children made. I loved the tradition of everyone opening one gift each as everyone else watched and waited for their turn.

Clint acted like Santa and picked a gift for each of us. Everyone had a pile of gifts with their name on them. Clint woke early and set aside the gifts for those who were not yet present.

Life is better in the memory of Christmas 2003. I am grateful that my determination to enjoy the moments created memories. The promises I made and the vows I kept directed my actions in life. I vowed to care for my children and stay the course in my marriage until I could correct the mistakes of my past. I remained hopeful the new year would bring a solution to my financial mess.

View my special message by scanning the code below
OR go to: https://qrco.de/1_NeverEverAgain

Chapter 2

Raiders Lose, Buccaneers Win

Marriage vows were a contract that I honored when I was married to Terry. I worked diligently and faithfully to be the best wife I could be. My vows were with my husband and God. 1 Corinthians 13 was the verse the justice of the peace read at our wedding.

> *"Love is patient, love is kind. It does not envy, it does not boast, it is not proud. It does not dishonor others, it is not self-seeking, it is not easily angered, and it keeps no record of wrongs."*

I was able to keep my vows to God better than I could to my husband. Honoring Terry while he was drinking, snorting lines of cocaine and cooking crack in a spoon was impossible. Being a good wife—patient, kind—meant doing everything I could to keep the peace in our family. I kept our arguments behind closed doors in our home and at the office. He would promise me the sun and the stars. He was super manipulative. Life with him was a trap of lies. I prayed and held onto hope that tomorrow I would wake to a better day.

I woke to the reality of our increasing debt load. I also saw the beauty of my children and kept on fighting the pain, shame, anger, and betrayal. Their love reminded me that I needed to fight to survive. I knew that bitterness and anger were seeping into my veins. Headaches became a normal until migraines began to force me away from the light into the relief of darkness. Sleep helped reduce the pain. Worrying about when Terry would return from another bender and how I would keep our sinking corporate ship afloat stopped me from sleeping peacefully.

Sleep deprivation prevented me from resting. I rarely slept for more than four hours without numbing my brain with two or three joints filled with marijuana. I woke from the heavy fog of a drug induced sleep with a dull aching headache that was ready to grow into another morning migraine. I swallowed Tylenol and Motrin with my four o'clock morning coffee hoping that the pain would fade before the sun rose.

Though Terry disappeared several times each month, he did not once go missing for more than 72 hours on his benders. I could never formally report him to the police as a missing person. I sent text messages to the team of foremen and job superintendents informing them that he still wasn't home. His sister and mother called to check if he had come home yet. I avoided their calls until I drove the children to school and began my day at the office.

The office was the command station for the battlefront that I continued to fight. I collected money due from completed contracts and paid bills always making the best decisions I could in his absence. Each time he returned from a bender; he reprimanded me for, "fucking everything up like a retard." His insults were always overflowing with cruelty. I began to fade deeper and deeper into the darkness of a depression that manifested into adrenal fatigue, hypothyroidism, endometriosis and uterine cysts.

The fatal blow to our home and financial health came during the 2003 Super Bowl weekend while we vacationed at Kimberly ski resort. The beautiful blue skies and snow on the British Columbia mountain scape offered hope for a peaceful family holiday. Clint drove shotgun with Terry in his black Dodge 350 diesel truck. Spencer and Jarett sat in the backseat. Chance, Emily and I drove in the battered blue minivan with the side door that needed to be slammed hard to close.

Terry's gambling that occasionally infused our bank accounts had become his passion. Sunday, Monday and Thursday football games were watched while wagers were made with his bookmaker. He mixed business with pleasure and made his bets with the same man who contracted us to pave his casino parking lots. His recent winning streak paid for the ski trip and funded his Super Bowl betting weekend.

I skied with the kids while Terry and Clint sat in the chalet lounge and watched the 37th annual Superbowl. Terry wagered on first, second, third and fourth quarters. His bets grew with each quarter. The Buccaneers defeated the Raiders by the score of 48–21, tied with Super Bowl XXXV for the seventh-largest Super Bowl margin of victory, winning their first-ever Super Bowl. His Raiders wagers cost us hundreds of thousands of dollars. Betting on the underdog with the big odds wasn't a win at all.

We returned home in silence. Days later the Canadian Revenue Association (CRA) called in their debt and seized the company bank account. The overdue taxes were confiscated legally. We could no longer pay our mortgage. The castle crumbled and we were forced to sell.

We moved into the eight-hundred-square-foot home that we called *the little house*. The home that was once our first home became our now home. Renters were evicted, curtains were hung, holes in walls were repaired and rooms were repainted. I cried myself to sleep alone while Terry numbed the pain with whisky, cocaine and crack. I also chose to embrace the new beginning and help myself.

Self-help books and audio recordings became my priority as I renovated each tiny room. I decorated Emily's room with the characters from the Hundred Acre Wood. Winnie the Pooh, Tigger, Eeyore and the gang brought love to life on the walls of her room. I read "The Tao of Pooh" by Benjamin Hoff during the three months that I primed, sketched and painted.

I learned many lessons. I understood that the master has no possessions. The more she does for others, the happier she is. The more she gives to others, the wealthier she is. I understood that the Tao supports not by forcing. By not dominating, I lead. I celebrated each lesson learned with more self-care. I enjoyed walks, meditating, praying and hiking in the forest that surrounded our acreage.

Terry's business partner Keith tightened the reins on his business agreement and the company they jointly owned. Keith intervened and demanded that Terry get help and overcome his drug and alcohol addiction. Drug addiction affects every area of life including finances, mental health, relationships and physical well-being. Terry committed to losing weight and exercise. He shed some pounds and gained some confidence. He didn't attend Cocaine Anonymous meetings or seek out counselling. Sadly, this wasn't the first attempt at intervention.

One year before, in 2002, after Terry's birthday, a bold family intervention was held in the house on Manor View Crescent. When the family celebrated his birthday the growing concern for his health increased. He had been celebrating the week before with another three-day bender. He looked gravely ill when Leslie, his sister, Heather, his mother, and her husband, Rollie came to share birthday cake at our home.

Once again, my phone rang with calls of concern for Terry. This time I answered and listened to Leslie who was determined to do something about her brother's problem. The fear was that he would continue using drugs and alcohol until one day he didn't come home. The worry was that one day someone would be identifying his body at the police station or morgue. The knowing was that something had to change, or nothing would change.

A few weeks later, Leslie organized an intervention and staged it in our home. I was terrified and knew that the backlash could possibly leave bruising marks on my body and leave more scars in my mind. I prayed that he would hear the love in his family's voices and act on the opportunity for rehabilitation. I hoped and concentrated my thoughts on a positive outcome. I researched rehabilitation facilities in Alberta and British Columbia. I was ready with a folder filled with printed pamphlets.

Heather understood the importance of the intervention and attended with Rollie. Her brother, Sonny, and his wife, Francis, came too. We sat in my living room, joined together with a common goal—making Terry admit he had a problem and convince him to choose us over the drugs. Terry's sister led the conversation and asked everyone to share their concerns. We told Terry how much he mattered. He listened and made promises. He said he would consider looking into a recovery program.

After everyone left, I was punished. He told me that I needed to mind my own business. He warned me that if I ever tried to organize another intervention, I would be the one who needed recovery. Terry told me I would regret opening my mouth. I was afraid that the boys would return home with Emily and that they would hear him. I knew better than to argue and make a bad situation worse. I turned to leave the living room and go to my bedroom. When I walked away from his angry rant, he pulled me back by my hair. When I cried, he told me to stop being a fucking baby and to grow the fuck up.

I wanted to scream and fight back. I wanted to walk out the door and never come back. I wanted to phone a friend and ask to come over. Instead, I went to the bathroom and splashed cold water on my face. I quickly changed into my pajamas so that I could cuddle up with Emily and read her one of our favorite stories.

I heard the front door slam. I wondered if he left. When I walked out of my bathroom, Jarett was waiting with Emily. He had helped her dress in her pajamas. "Emily's ready for story time. I put the book on her pillow." He hugged me and whispered in my ear, "Dad said he was going to get smokes."

I carried Emily to her bedroom and saw the book, "Love You Forever" by Robert Munsch on her pillow. We cuddled and read until she fell asleep. I kissed her on the cheek, turned off the light and carried the book to the living room. I read it one more time and prayed to my angels. I knew they were listening.

I couldn't talk to my friends because no one ever saw the side of Terry I did. They just didn't believe me because he was always the life of the party and helped when someone needed something. He could be the most loving husband in public, but in private my life was much different. Bruises aren't just physical but they're the ones people believe. Emotional ones are hidden from everyone but the one bearing them. I couldn't possibly admit that daily insults, weekly cruelty, and lonely nights were my normal life. After a while, I convinced myself that what he said was true. I was no longer the woman I once was. I lost my strength and independence. I had become comfortably numb to his insults. I stayed even though I wanted to go.

"No one will ever put up with your shit," he would always say, and I'd believe him. And when he'd tell me, "You are damaged goods, and you can't ever leave." I stayed for one *more day*—that would turn into months. I couldn't get out. I felt like the defeated Buccaneers.

View my special message by scanning the code below
OR go to: https://qrco.de/Raiders_Buccaneers

Chapter 3

Scandalous

I learned to speak my truth through writing words while my hands shook. Even though I was afraid of being judged, I was willing to escape from the shallows where I hid my scandals. I was uncertain as to what shame needed to be forgiven. So, I took a few moments to connect with my breath to quiet my mind and find the memories that wanted to be heard.

I remembered getting my hair ready for the first day of grade ten. I curled my bleach-blonde, poker-straight hair just like Farrah Fawcett's. I stood at the mirror imaging exactly what it would feel like to see my friends. As I put on my mascara, concealer, eyeshadow and lipstick, I listened to my favorite songs on the Sony Walkman that I'd bought from the money I earned working as a receptionist at the Edmonton Public Library. I played songs that inspired me from my heavy-metal playlist and sang along. Quiet Riot was one of my favorites because I loved their loud, lyrical, defiance and felt like a rockstar when I listened to their powerful Metal Health (Bang Your Head) prose.

With my headphones on, I walked the ten blocks to school as I sang, "Well, I'm frustrated, outdated. I really want to be overrated. I'm a finder, and I'm a keeper. I'm not a loser, and I ain't no weeper. I got the boys to make the noise. Won't ever let up, hope it annoys you!" The empowering lyrics helped me feel confident about my first day of school at M.E. LaZerte High School.

I envisioned myself walking up to the podium accepting my valedictorian award as I walked into the front doors of my new school. My knees buckled when I saw the mass of students standing in line at the main hall waiting to get into the office for their class list. I looked up at the clock and saw that I had seven minutes before first period.

Two minutes passed and then the buzzer sounded warning that I had five minutes to get to class. The main hall emptied within thirty seconds, and I was in a line of less than fifty students. Before me stood four lines each designated for a different alphabetical grouping, A-F, G-L, M-T, U-Z. I walked forward into the empty U-Z line and spoke to the lady behind the desk. "My name is Nancy Natalie Walters."

She glanced through the envelopes in front of her and pulled out an envelope with my name on it. "You better hurry up. You're already late for class."

I opened the envelope and saw that my first class of the day was English. I was excited to begin studying the lyrical prose of higher learning. I located the room number, asked for directions and danced up the stairs.

When I got to the door it was closed. I took a deep breath, knocked, opened the door and prayed. Before me sat a classroom of students that I did not recognize. My hands began to shake more than my knees as I walked through the doorway.

The teacher glanced up and told me to take a seat. I walked to the back of the class, sat down, took my headphones off and opened my backpack. While she continued to take attendance, I remembered that I had one mission which was to achieve honors marks and fulfill the entrance requirements for the University of Alberta creative writing program. My mom reminded me, "You'll never get into university with marks like this," each time I brought home a report card with marks under eighty five percent.

As the teacher continued to the end of her list, I panicked because she didn't call my name. She told anyone whose name was not on the list to raise their hand. I lifted my hand and told her my name which she wrote on a piece of paper in front of her.

Then she stood, walked to the black board and wrote, "English 30" with chalk. I was in the wrong class! I stayed frozen in my desk, deaf to her words unable to speak a single syllable.

When the bell rang to announce the end of class, I put my binder in my backpack and left the room. I found the nearest bathroom, entered the stall, sat down and opened the envelope with my class list. Sure enough, I had gone to the wrong room. I promptly pulled off my skintight jeans, peed, prayed and looked at my shaking hands.

The next bell rang announcing the second class. I looked at my list and saw that math was next. I pulled my pants up and told myself that I had to get to that class on time.

I made it to math class on time and was grateful to sit next to my friend John from junior high. I began to feel better when the teacher took attendance, and my name was on the list. Class progressed without any further problems. The bell rang and I walked out feeling a huge sense of relief.

John was waiting for me in the hall leaning against the wall with a huge grin on his face. He handed me a piece of paper and laughed, "Walters you missed English!" My worst nightmare came true because the biggest mouth in junior high had discovered my secret. I begged him not to tell anyone and within minutes knew it was already too late.

"Wow, you missed your first class," and then "Epic fail Walters!" followed by laughter. I felt humiliated, shamed, betrayed and ready to cry.

Instead, I turned to John and told him he was an absolute jerk. I proceeded to my next class and finished the morning distracted and unable to concentrate. I felt like the entire school was talking about me and all I wanted to do was go home.

When lunch came, I went to the mall across the street and sat with a couple of girlfriends. We shared fries, gravy, root beer, malts and talked about how stupid boys were. We walked back to school together and made a plan to have lunch together the next day.

The afternoon went by without any further drama, and I went home to soothe my hurt ego with marijuana and afternoon soap operas. When my mom got home from work, she asked me how my day was. I told her everything was good and that I had lunch with my girlfriends.

The humiliation of my first day affected my self-esteem and focus. I lost interest in math, biology, chemistry and history. The only class that kept my interest was English and I seldom attended because I spent more and more time at the mall skipping school.

I managed to escape getting caught for my extensive absenteeism by hiding the mail school sent home. I enjoyed truancy until my guidance counsellor contacted my mom in the third semester for a meeting.

Mrs. Walker the guidance counsellor sat with my mom and I to explain the grave issue that I had created. Even though I was passing, my grades would prevent me from continuing with the matriculation program. She suggested that I have a skill assessment completed to see what my career aptitude was. According to the tests, I would be better suited to accounting and business studies.

Even though I was angry that I got caught skipping, I felt like we figured out a fair, doable plan together. She helped me understand that if I took English again in summer school, I would be able to still study the literature I enjoyed. She kept an eye on me for the rest of the year, reported any concerns to my mom to avoid any more scandalous behavior and helped me see that I could make better decisions.

Summer school was a godsend that skyrocketed my success in writing because the teacher focused on grammar, sentence structure, punctuation and paragraph composition. I used the skills I learned to help me do well in all my business classes and graduated with honors in business.

In my final year of high school, she helped me find scholarship opportunities and complete my college application forms. Furthermore, she taught me that one person can make an incredible difference in a child's life. She helped me develop my belief in my inner strength, work through challenging situations and stay resilient to my desire to further my education after high school.

1987 was a year for great beginnings and incredible opportunities. I graduated from M.E. LaZerte High School with honors in business and a scholarship from the Edmonton Business Women's Association for The Most Likely to Succeed. Following in my mother's footsteps, I began my training in Secretarial Arts at the Northern Alberta Institute of Technology (NAIT).

View my special message by scanning the code below
OR go to: https://qrco.de/3_scandalous

Four Brothers

My career in motherhood began in the summer months of 1992. I became pregnant with Jarett, my first son, a few months after I received my acceptance letter to the University of Alberta. My plan had been to advance beyond my career as the Staffing Officer at Gainer's Meat Packing Plant. I designed a blueprint for success and was excited to study labor arbitration. My ambition was to find a way to guide management and union towards peaceful resolution. God had a different plan for me.

Jarett's name means noble warrior. His birth was the first trauma he experienced. My back labor began at home two days before his birth. After twelve hours of intense lower back pain, I insisted Terry take me to the hospital. Upon arrival, the student doctor examined me and announced I was seven centimeters dilatated. Nitrous oxide, commonly known as laughing gas, was the only pain medication I used to ease labor.

When Jarett's heartbeat began to drop indicating that he was in distress, the doctor began to take emergency measures. My cervix refused to soften, and the doctor began the painful process of membrane stripping to ripen my opening. At the same time, Jarett's heartbeat began to drop further. The doctor applied a suction cup to his head as the first attempt to coax his body from mine. When that method failed, he used forceps to grasp his head and guide him out.

As Jarett's heart rate dropped even further, the nurse told me I had to push, or my baby would die. I pushed with all my might and gave birth to my beautiful son. While the doctor delivered the placenta, the nurses ensured that his vitals were good.

The doctor then told me he would have to numb the area while he stitched me up. Fifty-two stitches and ten staples were required to repair my opening. I laid on the bed with only one concern. Was my baby, okay? The doctor assured me he was a happy healthy baby boy.

When they laid him in my arms, I was shocked to see his bruised face, and a large hematoma on his head. His soul looked at me through hazel brown eyes as though to assure me he was okay. I fell in love and every minute of pain dissolved. I learned that the pain I experienced in birth was temporary. Being a mother was a lifelong blessing.

Sadly, there are wretched memories that have tarnished Jarett's beautiful birth. I can still remember the smell of whisky on this father's breath the day he picked me up from the hospital. Terry justified abandoning us in the hospital for two days while he got drunk. Celebrating the birth of his son was the excuse he used for his first 48-hour bender.

Chance, my second born son, came gently into my world three years and two months after Jarett. His name means good fortune. He loved being in motion and slept best in the car. When he struggled to sleep as an infant, I would drive around our neighborhood until he fell asleep. Then, I would transfer him into his crib, place my hand on his torso and sleep on the floor. If I tried to sneak out to my own room, he would stir and wake.

I learned to adapt to the challenges and embrace the precious moments. I set up a mattress in Chance's bedroom on the floor next to his crib. The sound of his breathing was music, and I enjoyed the song.

My two stepsons, Spencer and Joshua, have been in my life for over twenty-five years. Spencer became a part of my journey in the summer of 1992 one month after I found out I was pregnant with Jarett. Terry brought him from Saskatchewan to Alberta to spend time with him in Edmonton.

I was not living with Terry. When I told him I was pregnant with Jarett, he said, "I didn't sign up for this." I packed my clothes into two black garbage bags and moved in with a friend.

A few weeks after Spencer came to visit, Terry called me because he needed a babysitter. Feeding Spencer McDonalds for breakfast, lunch and dinner had created stomach issues and he needed a caregiver while he went to work. I babysat for a couple weeks and moved back in within a month.

Spencer spent summers with us until grade six when he moved in permanently. When his teacher identified that he was struggling with reading, I met with her to see how I could support him. Together we created a plan that ensured he would be able to improve to grade level. I read with Spencer every night and within a year he improved five grade levels in reading.

Joshua came into my life in 1994, like an unexpected gift wrapped in a red bow. He was four years old and uncertain as to how to process his new father. Josh's biological mother had chosen a different man to be his daddy. When their relationship ended, Ron, the first father Josh knew, demanded a DNA test to prove he was the father. The test proved that he was not the father. The man who was Terry's best man when he wed Spencer's mother Christine suggested that Terry be tested. The DNA test confirmed he was Joshua's father.

I fell in love with Joshua instantly. His red hair, dancing eyes, and shy shrug were adorable. When Terry questioned what to do about the situation, I told him that Josh was part of our family. I became the go-between Terry and Joshua's mom Merritt.

I loved sitting around the dining room table with all four boys signing agenda books and ensuring homework was completed. I made charts for the walls and created reward systems to help them see the value of diligent work.

I struggled with my role as stepmom knowing that parenting Spencer and Joshua was Terry's responsibility. A healthy relationship would have been the wife supporting her husband in parenting instead of being the most involved parent. The responsibility of ensuring that each son got to school on time, with homework complete and lunch packed while organizing their evening sports events was a full-time job. The expectation that I would still meet all of the administrative responsibilities in the construction company we both worked for led to adrenal and chronic fatigue.

When I complained to Terry, he told me it was my job as a mother to make sure I take care of him and his children. My doctor warned me that if I continued to ignore my physical and mental health, I would be hospitalized. My struggle with endometriosis had led to dangerously low levels of iron. Each month I went for blood tests, the doctor suggested magnesium, b-complex vitamins, zinc, and time away from Terry.

Terry's response to my health challenges was, "My mother and sister did a much better job of taking care of their family." The only time off he approved of was going to bingo with Heather and Leslie. When I went, he complained that he had to stay home and babysit.

Spencer was the first of the merry band of brothers to advance into junior high. When he broke the rules, I was the parent who enforced the consequences. I was deemed the wicked stepmom who ruined his life. Terry taught him how to roll joints and party like a rockstar. He would belittle me, call me the "warlord" or "warden" and encouraged Spencer to do the same. At the age of sixteen, Spencer ran away from home. I learned to allow him to live his own life and told him he was welcome to come home for dinner.

Joshua's mother took him back to live with her in grade five. My heart broke as I witnessed him grow increasingly angrier. His mother's reckless lifestyle and lack of conscious parenting caused his rage to escalate. He returned to our family four years later after being expelled from school.

Terry decided that Josh would be better suited to working rather than education. I became his confidant and friend as he learned to landscape, operate heavy equipment and finish concrete. Spencer graduated from high school and joined Joshua's concrete crew. Jarett and Chance enjoyed working with them on weekends.

My sons each supported me differently when I struggled during the months after Emily's death. Chance brought me a pillow and a blanket when I cried on the bathroom floor. Jarett sat with me in the middle of the night when I couldn't sleep. Josh came over and rolled me a joint, took me to a movie, and allowed me to cry. Spencer reminded me of my strength and offered supportive hugs.

I am grateful that I chose a career in motherhood. There are so many beautiful memories that I have of being a mom. I loved the way each of my children fit perfectly into my arms. Days at the park, walks on the beach, camping trips and rides in the boat were all better because my children shared the moments with me.

FOUR BROTHERS

View my special message by scanning the code below
OR go to: https://qrco.de/4_FourBrothers

Chapter 5

Tales of a Battered Beauty

I was a mother, daughter, grandmother, and forever friend. I loved seeing all the possibilities each day brought as I gazed at the world around me. I saw the world through pure love. I was born with a purpose and creating through writing helped me voice this mission.

Counselling helped me understand the cycle of abuse. Abuse became battery when one more time became a second assault. I did not recognize that I was a battered woman until I heard another woman explain the difference.

My counsellor also encouraged me to pursue my desire to continue my spiritual education. I discovered through Spiritual Response Therapy (SRT) and Akashic record readings that I chose my parents, children, marriages and experiences to help me heal and become a better version of myself. Akashic records are the repository of every thought, word, and deed of every living being, good, bad, and awful, in all times; past, present, future. Within my records I saw that I chose the perfect family for my healing mission: loving, supportive, damaged, dysfunctional, and unaware of their self-destructive patterns.

My mother was supportive and loving. She had also experienced trauma and struggled with letting go of the past pain of her divorce. My father was also supportive and loving. His recovery from alcoholism was a daily journey that helped him stay sober. My journey of self-discovery and recovery was a mixture of letting go of the past pain of divorce and recovery from drug addiction. I hid in the shadows of shame for years afraid to tell my story. Like me, my parents hid in their own shadows of shame. Together we created the illusion of a picture-perfect, *Little-House-on-the-Prairie* happy family.

My mother's family avoided talking about alcoholism, sex, adultery, obesity, abuse and any subject that was outside the safe zone of dinner table talk. These topics were not to be discussed when children were present. Problems were swept under rugs quickly before company came over. Secrets were buried deep so the neighbors didn't suspect that adultery existed.

I watched my mom struggle with emotional pain and turn to fellowship within the church to help her heal from feelings of betrayal, anger, guilt, and depression. She kept the truth of the details of her marriage, separation, divorce and ensuing anguish from me. When I unexpectedly found the box of letters my father and mother wrote to each other, I was thunderstruck. My immediate reaction was uncertainty because I didn't know if reading them was going to cause me harm or help me heal the anger and resentment I held against both of my parents.

My mother lost trust with her husband and though they tried, they could not rebuild their relationship. No one explained how or why my parent's marriage broke down. I tried to understand why mommy and daddy didn't live together with my seven-year-old mind while I wandered in my Oma's garden. I looked at the birds and the bees, picked flowers and pressed them in books that I read under the apple tree, listened to my Oma and Opa talk and decided that I had done something wrong.

My father's family denied alcoholism, abuse, drug addiction and battery. Even though my father started drinking when he was a teenager and left home to escape his father, no one talked about it. When my cousins were molested, there was silence within the family. Abuse and battery were not topics discussed at dinner. Shame was hidden as we loved each other through our painful experiences. We did our best in a world that didn't know better.

I did not see my father's struggle because he lived in a city hundreds of kilometers away. The cards he sent me offered love and nothing to explain his absence. He found a new wife and created another family that offered him love. I didn't understand why he chose them and not me until I was a teenager.

When I met Rita, my stepmother, and her two sons, Richard and Michael, I saw the family I never had. I witnessed the love they created and the festive lifestyle that booze fueled within a blended family that had their own share of emotional pain. I felt like I had finally found the answer to my questions about my mother and father's failed marriage. My father was friendly, outgoing, adventurous and exciting which didn't fit my mother's faith-filled, structured, quiet and peaceful lifestyle.

My life has been a kaleidoscope of pain, trauma, abuse, addiction, battery, and beauty. I am humble and do not compare my trauma. My pain brought me to my healing, and I am grateful. Each day I practice resiliency as I walk up the rungs on my trauma ladder. My trauma ladder is a jagged staircase that began with a childhood near-death experience.

When I was only days old, I became very ill. My teeny tiny newborn body struggled with a life-threatening infection that caused severe diarrhea. Neonatal diarrhea can be fatal. My six-pound, three-ounce body began to lose weight. Intravenous lines and tubes were hooked up to my little hands, arms, feet and scalp. My parents kneeled in the hospital chapel when the doctor suggested they pray for a miracle. My body healed and I became their miracle.

I know exactly how I felt, what I saw, why I chose to live and the impact I would make in this world. The steps I took to uncover the roots of my beginning and move past skepticism through verification was an intricate design that took over a year to complete. Hypnosis was the entry point that helped me relive the experience of being in my mother's womb. Later, transcendental meditation helped me activate and then release the trauma associated with my parent's divorce.

I learned of my molestation while in a clinical hypnotherapy session. Forgiving the man who molested me became easier as I processed the experience during hypnosis. I am at peace now and am fully aware of how this experience influenced my actions and feelings. I understand why I fiercely protect my children. I know why I passionately speak my story and share my experiences.

Abandonment, my own addiction to cocaine and crack, battery, and betrayal were the ladder rungs that I climbed in my twenty-five-year marriage. Each step carried pain and emotional baggage. I fashioned scarves loosely around my neck because if I wore them tightly, I flashed-back to when my ex-husband tried to strangle me. I sat in restaurants facing the door to make sure I could see who was coming in. I was only able to sit with my back to the door when I was with one of my sons. I was glad that I realized I needed help to deal with my suitcase full of issues.

View my special message by scanning the code below
OR go to: https://qrco.de/5_Talesofabatteredbeauty

Chapter 6

Prescription for Strength

Emily began attending pre-school four mornings a week in September 2006. I was finally allocated time to do whatever I wanted. The problem was that years of isolation had left me without any purpose other than being a mother.

I was purposeless and sad. Pretending that I was happy was the equivalent of putting butter on moldy bread—it may look better, but it was still rotten. Rotten bread, rotten relationships, and rotten careers cannot improve without a prescription and then a probiotic.

I wanted to be like all the other moms who scurried excitedly to the gym, made coffee dates, dashed to the spa or did whatever their heart desired. Neither Spa Lady nor Sturgeon Athletic Club could coerce me into their lair. I had tried to two-step in the steel jungle where workouts condition the body into a shape other than bloated, flabby, weak, and vulnerable. I felt both inadequate and fake every time I stepped into a gym. I needed to find somewhere I had more of a connection.

I had failed to connect with the fit mothers in my neighborhood because I felt fat. When I became a mother, I abandoned the fit, toned, confident and brave woman who ran through the river valley every other day. I watched enviously as they ran by my yard. When they waved, I pretended not to see them.

33

I was afraid they knew the happy life I pretended to live was a lie. I was angry, exhausted, bitter and wise enough to know that I had created the life I was living. My inability to set boundaries for myself had allowed Terry to determine my daily schedule and workload.

I knew this was my opportunity to use my free time wisely. I desperately wanted to create a body that would not fail me when it was time to flee. I knew I had to strengthen my muscles with the same dedication that I had trained my mind. I needed to train to be a worthy opponent in our inevitable divorce. If I needed to pack the car with the kids and leave, I wanted to be ready to run.

Yoga seemed like a prescription that might give me enough strength to walk to the lawyer's office, open the door and ask for help. Meditation might help me breathe into my fears and face each challenge.

Even though I was uncertain about the exactness of how I would escape, I knew that I must. I was ready to create a better me and would no longer settle for less than I deserved. My desire was greater than my fear.

I chose the yoga studio on Perron Street in stylish St. Albert because it was near my best friend Tracy's nail salon. I had walked by it many times during the summer months afraid to stop, open the door and walk up the stairs. Today was different. I knew that if I faced one fear now, I would be able to face another later.

When I opened the door to the studio, I felt like I was at the stairway to heaven that would take me away from the hell of my marriage. Walking up the stairs felt great because I was doing something to change my life.

As I walked down the hall toward the studio, I heard a soft trickling of water and smelt the faint aroma of patchouli. When I entered, a kind middle-aged woman welcomed me with a smile and asked my name. I told her it was my first class. She passed me a clip board and asked me to take a seat and fill out the new student form.

I completed the form, passed it to her and waited. She smiled and told me to find a space for my mat. I walked into the classroom filled with seasoned yogis who sat quietly on their mats. I rolled out my mat and it thumped on the floor. I felt ashamed. I had no idea how to sit or what to do next. I sat and waited as I fought the urge to leave.

When the teacher floated into the room, I was intimidated by her confidence. I was terrified that she would look at me and see a failure. Instead, she began to speak like an angel. Her words were kind, gentle, soft and serene. She explained how to find a comfortable seated position and invited me to close my eyes. She guided me into the present moment.

"I am here," were here simple words of guidance.

I focused on her voice. My breath began to slow down. Then, without warning, my mind was filled with worrisome thoughts.

She spoke as though she knew exactly what had happened to me. "Take your to-do-list and place it on the space next to the mat."

I imagined all the things I had to do and scribed a quick note to myself. I imagined placing it next to me.

She continued, "If worrisome thoughts come, observe them and allow them to dissolve as they fade away."

When I forgot to breathe during class, I focused my gaze on the wall ahead of me. I listened to the teacher explain each pose and did my best. She told me to practice kindness to myself and others.

I learned that a one percent change to my thoughts created a better day. I enjoyed learning something new and embraced the opportunity to challenge myself. I felt like a warrior who could handle anything.

After class, I bought a month pass and committed to thirty days of wellness.

Then, I went to the grocery store and picked Emily up from preschool. She chatted all the way home about how much fun she had. I loved listening to her tell me all about her friends and what she had learned.

She told me her teacher let her pick her feeling from the chart that was at the front of the class. I enjoyed hearing her tell me about why she picked silly for her feeling. I laughed when she explained with funny faces and goofy sounds.

I was surprised when I pulled into the driveway and saw Terry's truck. He didn't normally come home in the middle of the afternoon.

I opened the front door and heard, "Fucking bitch will learn not to spend my money."

When he saw Emily, he smiled and opened his arms. She raced towards him, jumped up on his lap, snuggled into his arms and told him all about her first day in class.

I began unpacking the groceries that I had carried into the house. Terry stormed into the kitchen when he was finished listening to Emily. He demanded to know why I had used the credit card to buy a "useless fucking yoga pass."

I knew immediately that he was monitoring my spending. Nothing I said defused his anger. His response was simple, "Don't fucking do it again."

I realized that I had been given a gift. From that day forward I ensured that credit card purchases would be for groceries, office supplies, gasoline, and vehicle repairs. Any money spent on my escape would be cash.

View my special message by scanning the code below OR go to: https://qrco.de/6_PrescriptionForStrength

Chapter 7

Nose Candy

Holidays to Mexico fabricated a pivotal part of the façade of my marriage. Being the wife of a successful businessman meant showing up where he commanded and dressing as he dictated. The winter vacation he planned to Cancun in 2007 with a caravan of couples was the worst winter whiteout I'd endured in an endless avalanche of cocaine, Crown Royal whisky, and faceless whores.

Weeks before the vacation, Terry brought home a chronic infectious disease, caused by what he insisted was from only a blow job. His usual, "All the boys do it," was meant to dilute the fact that his fuckery could have left me permanently damaged. Terry's trolling on a weekend trip with the boys included limo service and hookers. I despised him and did not offer him a whisper of sympathy when he complained about the sores around his genitals. I told him if he wanted sympathy, look in the dictionary. You will find *sympathy* nestled somewhere between *shit* and *syphilis*.

I called the STD clinic and spoke to a counsellor who arranged for a visit the next day. I was tested for a full panel of sexually transmitted diseases, including HIV. He brought home a few and I received a shot in the ass for each of them. I did not want to vacation with him. My ass hurt from the injections and my heart hurt because of his relentless contempt. He kept downplaying the importance of his complete fuckery and condemning me for being heartless. He believed that he was a good guy who should be absolved of his sin because he told the truth. Jay's wife didn't know, so he told me, and Ken's didn't care.

I was enraged but silent. I did not speak to him until a couple days before the trip he had planned to Mexico. If he wanted me to go on the trip, the equation was simple: pay a fine to show admission of guilt or go alone and I'll tell everyone what a pig you are. Ten thousand dollars was his fine. He paid and warned me to keep my mouth shut. The money was an opportunity for me to hire a lawyer and finance a new beginning.

I preferred to vacation with my children because having them with me made me feel safe and loved. Knowing my mom was caring for them at The Little Acreage while we were away helped me trust that they would be well cared for. I was able to put on a smile and wave goodbye to the kids and get into the limo with Terry, Mr. Generous, who wanted to show off and pick up his family and friends in style. When I climbed into the limo his niece Krista wrapped her arms around me. She always gave me the greatest hugs. Krista's excitement was contagious, and I began to look forward to girl time, an excursion to Playa Del Carmen, picking seashells and swimming in the ocean.

When we got on the plane, Terry began ordering Crown Royal whisky as soon as the fasten seat belt light went off. The stewardess refused to serve him within the first two hours of the six-hour flight. I knew it was going to be another one of those nasty drunks when he called her a fucking cunt loud enough for the entire plane to hear. Luckily, he fell asleep, and his loud snoring created an even louder laugh from the stewardess who he had so rudely insulted earlier.

I sat and read "Excuses Begone!" by Wayne Dyer as my sad excuse for a husband snored and wheezed. Learning how to change my lifelong, self-defeating thinking habits was my focus. Even though I stayed married, I distanced my mind from his continual chaos and relentless recklessness.

I grew to despise every dinner, pool party, and excursion that Terry and I shared. Booze was a part of every social event we went to. Cocaine followed to help keep the party going all night. Sometime between dusk and dawn Terry ordered an eight ball of crack. An eight-ball of crack is about 3.5 grams, or one-eighth of an ounce. Mr. Generous would often order two eight balls so he could share with his friends. My heart broke as most of the people we travelled with stayed up late partying.

I went to bed early and slept in the other bed of our double queen suite. I woke early, walked on the beach, collected seashells and imagined my life without him. Formulating every detail of my life, exclusive from Terry, felt great. Planning my escape allowed me to disassociate from the fact that he often didn't come back to the room until mid-morning.

No one mentioned what happened at those late-night parties. Lipstick marks on his collar told me that he was still snuggling up to someone else. He tried to convince me all the lipstick stains were from his niece Krista. No one knew it cost me twelve thousand dollars to pay off the Mexican federal police so that Terry didn't get thrown in jail.

Our seven-day vacation ended with an embarrassing grand finale when we returned home, and Canada Boarder services interrogated several of us. Cocaine residue stuck to the lighters my ex-husband and his friends used. Crack was an adventure enjoyed by many.

NOSE CANDY

View my special message by scanning the code below,
Or go to: https://qrco.de/7_NoseCandy

Chapter 8

Daddy's Dirty Little Secret

Terry's generosity with his friends and family made our business appear to be lucrative. His ability to acquire new customers kept money coming into the corporate bank account. His ability to spend frivolously didn't keep enough for a steady, dependable bank balance. When his bank roll became large, Terry disbursed extravagantly. Money was spent on limousines, lavish parties, ringside seats, and weekends with the boys.

I hid my financial burdens from everyone. Leave-two-and-take-three was a decision I made with clothes I bought for our family when I couldn't afford them all. When my debit card was declined and I only had a little cash in the hidden pocket, I put back what wasn't necessary. I returned the dress and shoes I wanted to wear at Christmas dinner and chose a dress for Emily, shoes for Jarett and a jacket for Chance.

I hid emergency cash in the pocket I had on the inside of the diaper bag next to the number for the shelter I said I would call last week. Tracy gave me the number for the Edmonton Women's Shelter, and I agreed that I would call if he every abused me again. A few days later, Terry grabbed my long hair and pulled me back into the argument I didn't want to have. Instead of calling the number, I called Tracy's salon Elaine's Hair Den. I made an appointment with Bonnie for a haircut. She cut my hair into a short pixie cut. I didn't have the courage to call the shelter. It was the 1-800-WHY-AM-I-AN-ID-10-T "WHY AM I AN IDIOT" call I just couldn't make. Admitting that I remained married to the worst man instead of the best man was a truth that was harder to acknowledge than the little lies I chose to believe.

"Daddy's working out of town again, sweetie. I know you wanted him to be home for Christmas, but he bought you what you wanted," was the lie I told them to protect them from the truth I knew. Daddy was not working out of town. He was absent because he was on another bender in another house.

Months before I cut my hair, I learned the truth about Terry's dirty little secret. I drove him to pick up his truck at the crack house east of 66 street. He took a cab home after a bender and needed a ride the next day. I drove him to Lenny's place. He invited me inside to show me, "It wasn't really that bad. Lenny's a nice guy." The house was filled with whores— the whores your children tell you about while he was engaged to Gold-Digger Brenda, the next woman in a list of many who share in the pain he inflicts.

Telling the truth about the hell of my life was a choice I was unable to make. Instead, I became the secret keeper. Each undisclosed fact I buried increased the shame I felt. I was isolated in my home and within my mind. I developed a plan to escape the cage. Knowledge is power. I knew that the more I learned, the more I could earn. The more I could earn, the greater my capacity to create my own castle and escape his tyrannical prison.

Athabasca University, Canada's Online University, became my opportunity to study psychology and creative writing. I borrowed money from my mom to pay for the courses and studied with determination. Each course I completed increased my confidence. I readied myself for full-time university and willed myself to wait until Emily and I were able to escape together. I collaborated with universities in the United States of America. I spoke to campus counsellors and planned with purpose. When the time was right, I would be ready to earn my masters.

Terry hated me learning. I learned more. I defied him daily. I studied hard and achieved honors year after year. I became a learned scholar. My courage and confidence grew with each certificate and degree I earned. I celebrated my success with tattoos. I displayed my defiance with colorful creations on the body that belonged to me.

Terry hated my first tattoo, then my second, third, fourth and fifth. I have over twenty. Each tattoo on my body was a symbol of my strength and a piece of my story. I took back more of my power and control with each tattoo.

Mom and *Family First* adorn my left arm. Jarett, Chance and Joshua have tattooed their bodies with the *Family First* crest as well. Adam, my friend, has this crest tattoo too. Jarett was the first to ink his body with the crest and when Emily died, we all followed suit. Family First is my first family and my forever family.

Familia is tattooed on my right foot, a matching mark that bound me to my beautiful daughter-in-law, Jessy. We love travelling to Mexico. Planning vacations together allows us to enjoy creating a future together. Familia describes our extended family. My extended family is my second family.

DADDY'S DIRTY LITTLE SECRET

View my special message by scanning the code below,
Or go to: https://qrco.de/DaddysDirtyLittleSecret

Chapter 9

Is it Grease or Gravy?

Greystone had so many marvelous memories that began in the kitchen. Cooking was my muse as I heard my Oma's voice, and my hands became hers. My aging hands and her loving touch met in the space where memories joined. Love was the binding agent in food. Love bound my family together. My kitchen was a place where family and friends were always welcome.

Sunday diners were a special tradition that I shared with the Chaplin family. I would cook a huge dinner, invite Terry's family and allow the kids to invite their friends. Desert was always extra special because I made cakes, cookies, pudding and pies. I created special recipes that has been passed down from family or friends because they held a special space in my heart.

I am an exceptional cook, and my pies are known for excellence. I used my Oma's prize-winning pie crust recipe and created tiny lemon tarts. I loved to create perfect pastry flakes and a crack free crust. I was proud of my superb Sunday deserts and loved the joy my creations added to the excellence of dinner.

I loved to share my baking and often filled plastic containers for my friends to take home. Terry hated that I shared food with others. He wanted me to feed only his selfish desires. He would spitefully dig a spoon into the center of a freshly baked pie and eat a huge hole to stake claim to his prize. When I didn't bake enough pies to feed his hunger, he would call his mother and cry about how mean I was.

Terry's strange unwillingness to share food stemmed from a sibling rivalry with his brother David. He often told stories of how they would run home at lunch to claim the pizza their mother had cooked by licking the entire flat, open-faced Italian baked pie. Whoever arrived first won lunch because the other brother had to eat the spit-stained food or go hungry.

Terry was addicted to winning. His "win-at-all-costs" mentality was evident in his constant preoccupation with winning and achieving success. His compulsive and excessive need for victory continued to grow as he sought higher and riskier stakes to maintain the thrill of winning. His need to maintain power and control strained our relationship because he prioritized personal victory over marital success.

I got caught up in the cycle of addiction when I began to compete for his approval. The day he crowned Heather the queen baker I vowed to bake a better pie. The pie baking contest between wife and mother-in-law was fierce. My determination to win was intense.

Her specialty was raspberries. Mine was mixed berry and apple. Blueberry, strawberry, blackberry, and raspberry created a deep, passionate, royal purple. I combined all the berries and apples together with tapioca to bind. My pie crust was perfect—my Oma's recipe guaranteed flawlessness. Feeling my Oma's hands magically mesh with mine brought in a divine love that allowed me to compete peacefully and gracefully.

Each time Terry's mother baked pies for her prince, my irrational anger was immediately ignited within. I began to madly bake as though possessed like the vengeful father from *Thinner* Stephen King's horror novel, published in 1984 under the pseudonym, Richard Bachman. It's the story of Billy, a morbidly obese lawyer who, driving carelessly, kills an old woman while she was crossing the street. He escapes legal punishment, but cannot escape her father's curse, which he casts upon him by touching his cheek and saying "Thinner." After the curse is placed, Billy begins to lose weight rapidly and uncontrollably, regardless of how much he eats. In order to escape the curse, he must transfer the affliction to someone else hidden within a strawberry pie mixed with his blood.

My anger turned to understanding when I dropped a pie on the floor. Instead of acting from outrage, I began to laugh.

Instantaneously, I knew that what I wanted most was to be loved, valued, appreciated and understood. I declared the pie baking contest over and allowed Heather to enjoy the gift of Terry's love.

Terry responded to my lack of baking by rewarding his mother for her excellence with cash. He paid her one hundred dollars for each pie. He often ate alone, laughing and chuckling that Mommy loved him most. The sibling rivalry between Terry and his brother David fed Terry's need for power and control. Money was power and paying his mom fed his power-hungry heart. Keeping me on a leash without the funds necessary to escape was a continual act of control.

I baked pies for everyone. Baking brought me into a peaceful space where meditation met movement. Focusing on my breath anchored my mind in the present moment. Being grateful for my kitchen and my wonderful children filled my heart with happiness. My anger softened as I cooked with my children. My cupboards held all the ingredients I needed for baking and gratitude filled my heart. I freed myself from the disarray of my marriage with an attitude of gratitude. I focused on the beauty of each pie which created the perfect finale at our family dinners.

Having everyone gather around the table for Sunday family dinners made me happy. Turkey dinners were my favorite with mashed potatoes, gravy, stuffing, and turnip. Emily loved decorating the table with her handmade cards and gifts. My sons always helped me in the kitchen with Emily dancing and swirling. Music played in the background and laughter filled every room.

Gravy was my specialty, and I make it from scratch. My Oma taught me how to make it and, over the years, I have added my own special touches. Each dish I made was filled with love because I was cooking for people who appreciated me. Kind compliments and thankfulness was my reward.

When too much attention was paid to me, Terry would insult me. "What's for dinner wench? Did you make another toad stew?" My anger grew and destroyed the happiness that family and cooking created. I was never good enough and he reminded me daily. As we sat around the table one Sunday, he raised the gravy boat and asked, "Is this grease or gravy?"

I told him it was gravy, then stopped cooking for days. My broken heart cooked pizza pops, corn dogs, grilled cheese sandwiches and anything that delighted my children. Passive aggressive behavior became a norm in our dance.

My anger grew with every insult and insinuation he spat at me. Our dance became angrier and my responses vicious. I declared him my master and succumbed to being his slave. Sarcasm echoed in my words, "Yes Master Chap. Anything your say. Your wish is my command." My middle fingers raised in the air behind his back. Each combative conversation became a series of agreements. I was his slave, and he was the king.

I mistook the sparks of anger for power. Prisoners have little power when they allow themselves to be controlled by the insults their captors sling with savage spite. Believing that I could win the fight by pushing back was a joker's game. Foolish games add fuel to the fire of anger. The anger created more anger and Terry laughed.

View my special message by scanning the code below,
Or go to: https://qrco.de/GreaseorGravy

Chapter 10

Healing the Healer Within

My work family changed over the years because Terry appointed employees and business partners who fulfilled his need to dominate, party, fail and appear to be in control. We would often have family barbeques that included operators, office staff, business partners and customers. Most of the time I was able to stay in my role as the perfect wife until the day that I could not.

In 2008, after Terry didn't attend the company barbecue at our home, I began to become increasingly angry and excessively overwhelmed. I confided to Keith my friend and Terry's business partner that I was no longer sleeping more than four hours, smoking marijuana every night, waking the kids crying in my sleep and struggling to keep the peace in my marriage.

He confronted Terry and they decided that I would no longer continue to be an active participant in the daily operations of our construction company. Keith wanted me to spend more time focusing on my health and wellbeing. Terry wanted to me get the fuck out of the office and mind my own business.

I wanted to get as far away from the life I had created as possible. Being a working wife who spent her days and then nights with her husband had created a disastrous relationship because I could not manage the madness. Too many crack benders and cruel words had made it impossible to work with Terry in the company that I helped create. Hiring administrative assistance and book-keepers allowed for me to escape the cruel corporate world where my husband ruled. I entrusted the administration to two women who were also my friends.

Terri and Lori were both exceptional administrators who went the extra mile as my friends. They stood up for me when Terry was cruel behind my back and tried to guide me away from him. I stayed married to him not because I didn't know he was not good for me. I stayed because I if I fled, I would not be able to hide from his henchmen.

Few people knew the depth of his connections. Even less spoke about it. I knew more than I wanted to and kept my mouth shut. Snitches don't live to see their children grow up, graduate, attend college, marry and have children. I decided to continue my plan to create a stronger body and mind so that I was ready to escape when the time was right.

I returned to the mat each Monday morning and struggled with movements that felt strange. I was an imposter in a new land. Digging into the depth of each pose was difficult. My mind was filled with worries that I had made another mistake in trusting women. What if Terri and Lori accidently divulged my secrets like other women had before.

If Terry knew that I was going to yoga each day, I would have to pay the price for going against his warning to stop spending his money. Even though I had paid with cash, I still worried that he would see my vehicle parked in front of the yoga studio. To avoid the possibility, I parked behind the building near the library and walked the few blocks to class.

I followed the Vinyasa, a dynamic sequence of postures, that emphasized a flow of movements synchronized with the breath. When my feet fumbled, I glanced at my watch. Fear of getting caught in class because someone would tell Terry kept me in constant hesitation. I lost focus each time I glanced at the teacher, students, clock and my fat ass in the mirror.

When the teacher asked us to sit on the floor for the final set of asanas, I felt like a fake in a pit of despair. I was out of breath and frustrated because I could barely remember the movements I had performed. I was so hyper-vigilantly focused on what might happen, that I missed the opportunity to enjoy my practice.

My eyes flooded with tears that I refused to allow to flow. The last thing I was willing to do was allow myself to fall apart in front of everyone in the class. I tensed my muscles and forced myself to master the next pose. I would be damned if I would let this class end without getting one asana perfect.

The final pose had me lying flat on my back like a corpse. I began to relax into the mat and accept the resting pose. As my breath returned to a normal pace, the lady at the front of the class spoke. Her words of serenity brought me to tears. "Place your hands on your heart and feel the love. Understand that asana is to be in a seated position which is firm and relaxed. This is the work we do on the mat that is steady and comfortable. The practitioner is to be firm and relaxed. Many new students have trouble with this. If you feel unstable, panicky, ambitious, hurt and disillusioned, you may be approaching the postures the way you approach life. In our culture, results get all the attention, and the process is overlooked. Approach both your life and your postures with an eye to the process and let go of the results. Let go and let Gaia, mother earth, who loves and supports you. Trust that your life is unfolding exactly as it needs to be. Stand easy in all the postures of your life, firm and relaxed."

I felt a sense of peace during her closing meditation because I knew that I was not the only person who had struggled. I understood that I could be firm and relaxed at the same time as I trusted in the love of Gaia, the ancestral mother of all life. I connected with my breath and found a quiet calm. I was hooked because I had begun to understand why I needed to be here now. Learning to trust myself and the loving women in my life would help me move forward in the direction of my dream for freedom and a life without Terry.

I returned to the mat each week to practice with teachers who inspired me to relax in the pose and stop trying to ambitiously achieve perfection. I learned to let go of so much hardness inside my physical body which showed up as tension in my hamstrings, neck, back and mind. I desired to be much more and began to imagine the possibility of becoming a yoga teacher.

I focused on healing myself because I knew that in order to be a successful teacher I needed to focus on healing the healer within me. I understood that I needed to learn where my hurt was within my physical and emotional body. I also knew that I needed to continue to focus on my codependency which left unchecked could lead to me caring more about helping others than myself.

View my special message by scanning the code below,
Or go to: https://qrco.de/healinghealerwithin

Chapter 11

Daisy

On my fortieth birthday Terry planned a party. Friends and family came to Greystone and celebrated in our three-car garage. My heart was filled with memories of love, laughter, happiness and a dark knowledge. Once again mister wonderful had succeeded in making it look like he was a generous husband who adored his wife. The story he built was created to make him look good while he was having an affair with a woman who strolled the beaches of Kelowna.

Mister not so wonderful bought me a neon green Camero and presented me with $40,000. A few weeks later he demanded I lend $42,000 to his friend. When the money was paid back, he gave it to Terry.

I named the car poison ivy because she was green and not what I wanted. For years I dreamt of a convertible with a standard engine. The car he bought me was an automatic with a hard top. When I complained, he said I was being difficult. Nevertheless, I spoke to the sales manager and asked about selling it and purchasing the model that I wanted. He called Terry to discuss the opportunity.

Cars lose their value when they are driven off the lot. If we traded in the car, money would be lost, and I was to blame. Terry decided to keep the car for himself, and I was allowed to custom build the car I wanted. I was warned it would be the last car I would ever get from him.

57

DAISY

I designed my 2012 monarch orange convertible Camero exactly how I wanted with a standard transmission, Hurst shifter, leather seats, and racing tires. I added an electric horn that sounded like Bo and Luke Duke's General Lee. I admired the 1969 orange Dodge Charger from the Dukes of Hazard and wanted to replicate it as much as I could.

Finally, I had the car I wanted and named her Daisy. I felt like Maid Marion in search of her Robin Hood fighting against my captor The Sherriff of Nottingham. Emily and I drove around town pretending we were the good guys in Sherwood Forest just like the characters in Robin Hood. We spent hours driving around listening to music and laughing while our hair flew in the wind. The more I took back my power and control the better I felt. The further I drove away from Terry, the freer I became.

View my special message by scanning the code below
OR go to: https://qrco.de/11_Daisy

SCAN ME

Chapter 12

Murder of Crows

On August 24, 2011, Emily and I sat on the patio of our vacation home in Kelowna and created a vision board. I cut out pictures of yoga poses, graduations, scuba diving, and condominiums. I glued them onto a poster board and added a bold title in the middle "Time W.O.K." I explained to Emily that it meant time with-out-kids so that mommy could focus on learning to become a yoga teacher.

Trusting the universe and manifestation had become a passion of mine. I spent the early morning hours reading and attending on-line workshops about mindset, deliberate intention, the Laws of Spirit and reincarnation. I was so excited to be spending the next three months learning how to link asanas together and create classes for my friends and family to attend.

Jarett was remaining in Kelowna with his girlfriend Hailey and living in the guest house on the lakefront property we had rented for the year. They had secured jobs at the Okanogan Lake Resort in housekeeping and were excited to begin their new adventure as adults.

Chance had already returned to Edmonton to get ready for his first year of high school. Joshua and Spencer were busy adults with a fabulous circle of friends, jobs, steady girlfriends and aspirations of running their own construction company.

Emily was excited to begin grade five and was already planning sleepovers with her friends and spending time with her auntie and cousin while mommy went to school. I devised the perfect plan and was excited to return home to Edmonton the following week to prepare the kids for back to school. Beginning the next chapter of my life filled me with happiness, hope, optimism and gratitude.

Two days later, on August 26, 2011, I sat on the same patio as ten crows flew into our yard and sat on the branches of the dead tree next to the lake. I felt as though they were talking to me with their loud and rambunctious song. As a child, I watched my Oma chase them away with a broom yelling, "Flieg weg, du Teufel" which meant fly away you devil. She explained that they came from hell to eat the crops.

I looked at the murder of crows in the tree and saw the beauty of their black wings. I wondered why there were ten together. Crows have been grouped in murders since the late 1400s. A crowd of crows is called a murder because of the tremendous noise they make. Murder is associated with death. The ten in tarot symbolizes completion.

Emily was conceived on the tenth day of my menstrual cycle. I found out I was pregnant ten days after she was planted in my womb. I did not know she would be ten years old the day she died. There was no way I could understand the pain that I would endure nor the strength it would take to survive.

The manager of the El Dorado hotel called my cell to tell me of the accident. I did not hear the cell phone ring. The crow's song drowned out the chime. I saw the indicator light on when I walked back to the patio. I looked at the call list and saw that an unknown name had called. I sat down and checked my messages. I listened to the mysterious message and heard the words accident, Sea-doo and Eldorado.

I ran to the dock and called Terry on his cell phone. I told him about the message. He raced home in his boat. He was only minutes away. I tossed my phone to him so he could listen to the message. His face filled with fear. The phone was tossed back, and he raced to the dock at the hotel.

I sprinted back to the house. Nikita was playing with Aunty Breezy. I asked Breezy if she would watch Nikita while Tania and I drove to the Eldorado dock. I turned to Tania and told her there had been an accident. I grabbed the keys to my car. Tania walked to the door and blocked the way. She asked me for the keys and insisted it was better for her to drive.

Tania suggested we go to the hospital. I saw the ambulance lights as we approached the Eldorado Hotel and heard the silence. I asked her to turn toward the flashing red and blue lights. I knew I needed to go to the scene of the accident. My gut told me that no one was at the hospital.

I walked past the police, fire fighters and paramedics. I saw the crushed front of the Sea-doo and a man leaning over a body on the dock. Tania stopped everyone who tried to talk to me. I walked closer and saw Emily and Terry. I saw the dried blood around her long blond hair. I heard the words, "Our baby girl is gone."

I knelt on my knees and touched her face. I ran my fingers through her hair until I felt the tangle of dried blood. I closed my eyes and began to pray. I stayed until I was able to be the mother I needed to be for my son who survived.

I stood and told Terry I was going to find Jarett. I turned and looked for Tania to guide me on my way. We walked past the reporters and photographers who had gathered at the scene.

Talking to reporters while grieving the death of a child was an awful experience. Emily's father spoke to them while I stayed at the hospital with Jarett. When I read the news reports, my heart felt heavy. I saw her brother drove Emily to her death weaved into the reports over and over. Nowhere did I read that the boat swerved to miss Jarett's girlfriend and, instead, killed his sister. I struggled to not hate each and every reporter who told the tragic tale to increase their subscription rate. Each time I market my own products and services, I remember to sell what makes a difference in the world. I wonder what difference marketing tragedy makes.

Only the black, dark press knows why they line their pockets with tragic tales. Someone will read these words and take offence at the mediocre journalism they write. Someone else will read my words and feel the heartbreak of a mother.

I turned off the television and stopped looking at social media to heal my broken heart. I raised my arms up in the air and begged for an angel to guide me. Archangel Uriel, the angel of light, came and wrapped me in a blanket of love. He offered warmth during the cold days I sat in the hospital with Jarett. I sat in silence as he rested. I walked to the hall where my dad stood and cried on his shoulder. He held me in his arms and told me he loved me.

Terry walked Emily's body to the morgue. He witnessed her cremation and scrubbed the blood from the dock. He focused on her death while I focused on Jarett's life.

As parents we did what we needed to do. We walked in two different directions while doing our best to keep our heads above water. Our differences became apparent as we planned to celebrate Emily's life.

Terry met with reporters, police and the boat driver. He created an event to ensure that the world knew how much he cherished his princess. His party plans included renting the biggest boat he could find, t-shirts with Emily's picture, banners, a catered meal and pails of rose petals. The after party had a disc jockey, dance floor and plenty of booze.

I visited the funeral home with Tania, met with the undertaker, picked an urn and a starfish to carry Emily's ashes and signed the papers to declare her death. I stayed in the shadows while he stood in the spotlight talking to reporters.

Hundreds of friends and family travelled to support our family as we prepared to say farewell to the little girl whose life had touched so many. The lake house overflowed with friends, family, gift baskets, flowers and cards offering words of support. I read through hundreds of messages on Facebook while searching for a message to tell me that Emily had arrived safely on the other side of death.

View my special message by scanning the code below
OR go to: https://qrco.de/murderofcrows

Chapter 13

Stitches, Snitches, and Bitches

My head tingled on the very top as I began writing, an indication that my sweet Emily was present. Her fingers tickled the top of my hair. It was the sweetest, softest, most gentle touch. She reminded me that when I spoke about her dad—her daddy, her father—that I could speak my truth and remain kind. I promised I would do my very best, my dear.

I looked down at my left hand and remembered the day when eight-year-old Chance washed the dishes with three-year old Emily as I rinsed them in the hot water. We lived in *the little house*—eight hundred square feet kept us all together and captive within the utmost challenging situations. The boys understood the details of our financial decline. We had yet to recover from the financial downfall after the Buccaneers and Raiders Superbowl. Terry continued to play online poker. He insisted that poker was a gamble that he could win and recover his loses.

Focusing on all that I had allowed me to be grateful. Knowing all that I could change helped me stay determined as I found new ways to increase my understanding of spirit. I practiced gratitude and deliberately focused on being peaceful. I loved the way that, when we washed the dishes, I could look out the window onto the deck. It was a small deck, and I loved it so very much because I could sit and stare at the trees that surrounded our home. In the quiet moments when the children were at school, I wandered in the forest and communed with nature. I loved picking plants and flowers to decorate our home. The simple beauty of nature brightened each room and improved the energy. I yearned to learn more about herbal medicine and my walks fueled my growing curiosity.

Living at the Little Acreage in the Little House allowed for more ease and simplicity in my life. Instead of spending days cleaning the Manor View estate, I could clean the little farmhouse in a few hours. I was able to spend more time strolling in the forest and sharing time on the deck with friends and family creating celebrations and memories. I cared more about peace and less about whether Terry was home or not.

The day I washed dishes with Emily and Chance was not a special day or a birthday. There was absolutely nothing that indicated anything important. I was washing wax off a set of candleholders that were like a long-stemmed wine glass, but smaller in very hot water. I washed these because I didn't want my kids to get burned.

When I saw blood, I went into medical training-mode. I wiggled each finger, until I got to my middle finger.

Something was wrong.

I wrapped a paper towel around it, as I calmly walked into the living room, where Terry was. He was behind the computer, playing online poker, and when I interrupted him to show him my finger, he responded in a way I hadn't expected.

"Don't be such a fucking baby," he'd said. "Wrap it up with tape. It ain't so bad." He rolled his eyes and sniffed with disgust. I expected some compassion. I hoped he would respond with loving concern.

I replied, "I'm going to the hospital."

I changed the paper towel on my finger and wrapped tape around it to hold it secure. I readied to drive myself to the hospital, ensuring that all the boys and Emily were aware that I was going to the hospital to have the doctor look at my finger. Terry continued playing poker and telling me I was being foolish, and it'd be a waste of time. Emily insisted on coming with Mommy and I agreed, knowing that I would feel better if she was with me. I knew that Terry would be minimizing my injury and making cruel jokes. Emily cried when daddy was mean to mommy.

We drove to Sturgeon Hospital in St. Albert, the same hospital where she'd been born. I smiled at the memory of her amazing birth. Tracy, my best friend, arrived at the hospital without me calling her. She instinctively knew that I was in labor. Emily's umbilical cord was the longest that my doctor had ever seen. Our physical connection was the first sign of our special bond.

As we stood in line, I checked my phone for a message—an apology, some concern, something.

There was nothing. I was filled with rage. What would have to happen to me for Terry to step away from his precious poker and make me a priority?

The receptionist checked me in, then sent me to triage with Emily.

The nurse assessed the injury and mentioned surgery. Why would I need surgery for a little cut?

And then the doctor came in.

This wasn't a run-of-the-mill cut.

I went into immediate mom-with-a-kid mode. "Sweetheart, you're going to go color a picture with the lady at the front desk because Mommy's going to have a little visit here with the doctor."

Emily shook her head, "Nope. I'm going to stay here with you, Mommy. I want to watch."

There was absolutely no doubt or fear in that little trooper's eyes, so I had to put on a brave face and accept the inevitable—Emily wasn't going anywhere.

The doctor examined my hand. "Mrs. Chaplin, I am going to have to relocate your tendon."

I really didn't understand what he was saying. "Relocate? It's right there. Do you mean you have to *find* it?"

He nodded. "Your tendon has been severed and snapped back into your hand, so we're going to have to make a small incision to find it. I'm going to numb your hand, and everything will be fine."

Well, fuck a duck! This was going to require a little bit more of a calm demeanor than I'd expected. Emily was intent on watching, so I was determined to be brave.

Each needle he stuck into my hand burned like a third-degree burn on the inside, and I wanted to scream. I wouldn't even allow myself to wince because I didn't want Emily to know I was in pain. I simply smiled and looked at him as he continued to poke several needles into my hand.

Emily stood right beside the doctor and watched. "Wow, Mommy your brave!"

I smiled and watched as the needle moved into my skin. I was grateful that the freezing stopped the pain.

I left with fifty stitches. Some internal, some external, but, nevertheless, the middle finger on my right hand was definitely not just a simple tape-it-up-suck-it-up-don't-be-a-baby wound. As I drove home, the adrenaline that had kicked in was kicking out and I was getting tired. I just wanted to go home and rest in peace. I prayed that Terry had one of his temper tantrums and left home for a three-day-bender. I wanted peace and quiet. I needed a break from the chaos he created.

When we got home, it was time for Emily to go to bed. The house was quiet, so I could hear Terry snoring. Thankfully, he wasn't sitting at the computer playing, so I didn't have to deal with his disgusting behavior. Watching him sit at the computer wearing only his underwear and filling his mouth with candy and cookies while chugging a two-liter of coke made me nauseous.

Chance and Jarett were awake, watching television. "Mom, are you okay?"

"I'm okay, buddy," I replied to Jarett. "I'd really appreciate it if you would help your sister get ready for bed. Chance, you're going to have to get ready for bed by yourself."

I closed the bedroom door to muffle the sound of Terry's snoring. I laid down on the couch and closed my eyes and thought, payback is a bitch. I hope when Karma comes to pay you back it hurts more than my finger.

Karma came seven years later in 2012 about six months after Emily died. It was early in the morning. Terry sat at the long wooden table in our dining room. We were living in a home much larger than the eight-hundred-square-foot farmhouse.

The size of our home grew and so did the magnitude of our relationship problems.

Greystone was in Sturgeon County west of St. Albert in a quiet neighborhood. The 5,000 square foot home in a brand-new subdivision offered me hope for a new beginning. After years of rebuilding our finances, we qualified for a mortgage and moved into a new home. 2008 was the year that our new life started. The new life carried the same destructive patterns of weekend benders and cruel comments. What was different was that the heartache would break me.

Before Emily died my priority was creating a life that included more time WOK–With-Out-Kids—to allow for me to pursue a career in yoga, study aromatherapy, write this memoir and finally leave Terry. Without Emily and her laugher, nothing in the home made me happy.

I woke early the morning Karma came because I heard Terry's ring tapping on the kitchen table.

"Hey, bitch. Wake up. I need coffee." He was louder than normal, and he was pissed off.

Getting up and making him coffee was easier than it was to stay in bed. I put on my house coat and got up. The walk from the bedroom to the kitchen seemed to take hours, but it was only minutes.

What I didn't expect was to see him at the table with my journal wide open. I had been journaling for quite a few months as part of my recovery from decades of battery and the loss of a child. The death of a child is something that is quite difficult, and journaling was helping me. The practice that started when I worked through the twelve steps during my years of codependence counselling had taught me that writing helps me heal.

I turned the coffee pot on because it was ready to go. All he'd had to do was push a button, but he wouldn't. He didn't *want* to press the button; he *wanted* to pick a fight.

I waited for the coffee to brew as I listened to his breathing behind me. He was still tapping the ring. The big, red, ruby, showpiece, the professional poker player's winning trophy that he loved to wear. Terry had won one ring during a professional poker player's tournament. His big win made him look like a winner. The fact was he lost hundreds of thousands of dollars to acquire it. Our family lost valuable time together. His late-night poker playing took away from his ability to successfully manage our company. It was a showpiece I hated for a million reasons.

I poured two cups of coffee and sat down, choosing to be far enough away from him that he couldn't swing and hit. If he was going to swing, he was going to miss, and I was ready.

"I've been reading your journal," he said.

No shit, Sherlock, was what I wanted to say, but I didn't want to start a fight first thing in the morning. "Journals are private," I replied. "They're like diaries, and only meant for the person who wrote them to read."

"Well, then you shouldn't have fucking left it out in the open. I want to know if what you wrote is fucking true," he seethed.

I took a deep breath, and then responded with complete honesty. "Everything I wrote in there is true and from my heart."

He pointed his finger in my face so close just like a principal would, so I responded in the only way I knew how.

I bit that finger, and I bit it *hard*.

He screamed in pain as the blood dripped down his finger. "You fucking bitch! I'm going to need fucking stitches! You fucking cunt! When I get to the hospital, should I tell them my fucking dog bit me?"

I responded with complete calm, which I hadn't expected, as though someone else was speaking through me. "No, tell them it was your wife."

He didn't go to the hospital. He didn't need stitches. His pride had been hurt and his finger was bruised and sore. I had done just enough damage to ensure he stayed at arm's length. I felt such an incredible satisfaction and beamed knowing that Karma had come to pay back Terry.

"You will regret this," were the sinister words he spoke as he stormed out of the house.

Thirty minutes later my phone rang. I was not surprised to hear that he had driven directly to the office to showing everyone his wound. His intention was to tarnish my reputation. His plan backfired because the caller told me that he looked like a complete fool and the fellas he worked with were poking fun at him.

Terry did not return home that night. Instead, he chose to drown his sorrows with the boys. I wasn't surprised when he extended his escapade to a three-day bender.

Time away from him allowed me time to rid my home of the toxic energy we had created. I began by smudging with sage, cedarwood, sweetgrass, tobacco and Palo Santo. I loved how the scents combined to create a woody smoke with sweet undertones. As I walked from room to room with my abalone shell filled with smoldering sacred herbs, I repeated "Heal, Clear, Resolve" and allowed the smoke to cleanse, purify and clear all the negative energy. I smudged myself and asked my angels to surround me with their love.

I placed the shell back onto the silver tray that sat on my bedside table and began the second step. Opening every window and door allowed for the smoke to clear. I asked my angels to remove any and all destructive energies and replace them with peace. When I closed the doors, I heard my angels whisper, "Take the next step. Sit on cloud nine and you will find bliss."

I knew that I needed to work through the emotional trauma of my day because if I avoided my feelings, I would increase the potential for a migraine. I returned to my bedroom and sat down on my yoga mat. Burning sacred herbs brought in the perfect energy to enhance my meditation practice. Focusing on my breath allowed me to feel into my physical body. I felt a deep stabbing pain in the middle of my back and a heaviness in my chest. My heart chakra was blocked, and I needed to do the necessary step to return to love.

I began to breath deeper and focus on my ribs, chest, heart and middle back. After a few minutes, I knew exactly what I needed to do. I giggled because the angels guided me to my next action. I reached over to the bedside table, opened the drawer and took out my journal. I wrote, "Take the next step. Sit on cloud nine and you will find bliss."

Step 9 of the 12-Step program helped me repair my relationship with myself and relieve the burden of guilt and shame. I had made amends to my children because I knew that the ripple effects of abuse and addiction caused them pain. I accepted responsibility for my own volatile behavior and did my best to stay in a place of peace.

Writing letters in my journal helped me take responsibility for past actions and their impact on others. I knew that violence in relationships was dangerous, and I needed to do something to stop the rage. With my red pen I surrendered and began writing.

"Dear Terry, I am sorry that I lost my temper and bit you. I don't know if I can ever forgive you for all of the harm you have done to me. I am willing to try to find a way to mend my relationship with myself. Forgiving myself for staying in our marriage is very important to me. I know that I cannot heal my heart alone and am willing to allow my angels to help me. I can control my behavior better when I take the time to care for myself. I know that you can take care of yourself and that you do not need me. I am willing to release myself from the bonds of marriage with you."

I allowed the tears to flow and accepted that our marriage was over. I trusted that my angels would help us find a way to move forward in the directions of our dreams separately. I let go of the how and focused on what I could do in the now.

I closed my journal and placed it back in the drawer. It was a beautiful day to adventure into the wonderful world of uncertainty with gratitude, focused determination, acceptance and courage.

I turned on the shower and let the water run while I walked to Chance's room to wake him. I knocked on his door, "Sunshine, it's time to get up. It's a great day for a great day."

I honored my pledge to continue to take back my power and control and prioritize my health by enrolling in yoga teacher training. Completing the program helped me understand that my self-destructive patterns could be changed by practicing self-love. I recognized how often I habitually self-sabotaged my happiness and health because I was giving more to my marriage than I received in return.

I completed my yoga teacher training and set up a studio in the basement of my home. Teaching family and friends allowed me to share my passion in a safe space without having to sign a contract with an entity outside of myself.

View my special message by scanning the code below OR go to: https://qrco.de/stitches_snitches_bitches

Chapter 14

Lost and Found

Emily was often searching for something she had lost—little things that didn't mean something to anybody else and meant a lot to Princess Emily. She would scour her bedroom, her brother's bedroom, the kitchen and every corner of the house, searching for that one special treasure to take to school. She loved to make gifts for her friends and made a point of having a present for everyone because it was important to ensure no one felt left out.

Little Miss Sunshine was a bright, happy, smiling, dancing girl who loved to plan parties and sleepovers with her friends. School was the perfect opportunity for her to organize play dates with friends. She was the leader of the pack who guaranteed no one was left out of her weekend popcorn and movie sleepovers.

When she could not find her backpack that was filled with invitations for her friends, I would hear her stomp around the house in a rage blaming her brothers for hiding her things. The boys loved to tease her and sometimes picked up what Emily left lying around the house, putting it in her bedroom under her pillow or in a closet. If she was angry, the scowl across her brow was enough to make Jarett and Chance duck tail and run when she believed that they hid her prized possession. Watching her whirl around the house was like fireworks on the Fourth of July.

Many times, we would be at the school after class because Emily was looking through every single lost-and-found box for her favorite shirt, shoes, agenda book, or her entire backpack. When she couldn't find something, I always suggested she retrace her steps. I assured her that what was most important to her was not lost by saying, "We don't lose things, sweetheart; they simply get misplaced."

I would love to spend another morning frantically looking for her lost backpack instead of searching my mind for a memory to remind me how her hand felt in mine. The day after she died, I was forced to hear the words I hated. Kind sentiments from friends, family, neighbors and strangers pierced my heart like a surgeon's scalpel, "Sorry for your loss." I hated those words so very much because I had not *lost* my daughter; she'd been stolen from me. She'd been torn from my arms in the middle of the evening by the angel of death.

I felt like the boat driver had crawled up from the depths of hell and robbed her from me. Every time someone said, "Sorry for your loss," I felt the wound in my heart rip open and the blood flow directly from my veins.

When death comes, we share the words of comfort that we have been taught to use. We speak and write condolences and express sympathy to ease the suffering, sorrow, misfortune, or grief of another. The words that we use have such incredible power. Yet, no words can take away the pain.

When Emily died, the thought that she was in a better place helped until I missed her. I missed her every day. I struggled to want to stay on earth and suffer another hour without her. Yet, I knew there were more magical memories to be created and wonderful people to meet, because spirit showed me glimpses of my future when I slept. I understood that my other children needed me, and we were going to create a beautiful future together. I knew that staying with them would give me wonderful experiences and precious memories. I also wanted more memories with my daughter.

I could not get more time with Emily and because of her eternal love I was able to endure more pain. The cruel, hurtful words that would be spoken by the man I vowed to love until death do us part were expressions of his own trauma. I did not expect them and was shocked by the agony they brought to my life.

"I love you, but I'm not in love with you," are the words that Terry said to me in the hot tub the day that he decided our marriage was over. The heartbreaking moment was experienced by my sons because they overhead the conversation. I knew they heard when I heard the upstairs patio door slam. I saw the sadness in their eyes when I returned to the living room and sat down to talk to them about the traumatic event.

When Terry left, I found the strength to allow myself to focus on my own healing. I knew that healing my broken heart would take time. Journalling became my daily practice as I learned to focus on each painful emotion. I concentrated on one emotion each day and began with abandonment because it had been a constant in my life. I learned that sadness was the root pain of my feelings of shame, despair, betrayal, apathy and abandonment.

I shared what I learned with my sons to help them understand root causes of our generational trauma. I explained that the emotional effects of trauma are passed down from one generation to the next. I drew pictures of our family tree and showed the common pattern of addiction.

Within a few weeks, we were able to talk about the most painful times in our life. Our heartfelt conversations uncovered painful moments. One of the most agonizing was for the day that my son told me that Terry told him, "You killed your baby sister." I was instantly enraged and knew that the best course of action was to assure Jarett that he was not at fault for his sister's death.

The next day I researched options for emotional support to help Jarett. I was grateful that he was open to trying raindrop therapy which combined aromatherapy, essential oils and a specific massage technique. The powerful process helped him release some of his guilt and shame. He came home feeling more calm, peaceful, rested and willing to continue healing his physical and emotional pain.

View my special message by scanning the code below
OR go to: https://qrco.de/14lostandfound

Chapter 15

Castle of Hope

When I looked back in my memories, I see a day in the spring of 2014. I felt brave enough to pack up more of Emily's clothes. One minute I was folding her T-shirt and the next I ran to the washroom. I needed to escape the reality of her death. As soon as I entered the bathroom she shared with Chance, I saw her jewelry box and knew that I would never walk her down the aisle when she married. The engagement ring that she would show me would never exist. I felt like my heart had been torn from my chest.

How was it fair Terry was planning to marry another woman, and they would be walking toward their future while mine died. What cruel God could allow for him to marry his mistress? What sick plan had been created for so much unhappiness in my heart and home?

Chance knocked on the door. He asked if he could come in.

"Yes," it was the only word I could say.

He asked what he could do to help.

I asked for Emily's pink pillow and a blanket.

I laid on the floor until all the tears I was able to shed were cried.

When I was done, I opened my journal and wrote to both Terry and Gold Digger Brenda. I let my journal be a safe place for all my rage. I pondered my past with my pen. I demanded answers from a God I could not hear. Anger and rage blocked my ears from hearing.

I released the rage and saw the truth of my anger. I saw that Terry never once inspired me to find true happiness. He offered money from a heart that held no space for true love. I understood that he couldn't give what he did not have himself. I wanted more than money could buy.

I wished Brenda well. In the sacred space of my journal, I warned her to be wary of a man who cheats on his wife. I asked her to ask herself one question. If he cheated on his wife to marry you, will he cheat on you to bed another?

I owned my own part in the drama of life after divorce. I knew that I needed to move on with my life and build my own castle. I opened my phone and called a friend who built homes. I asked him if I could come and look at his show homes. He messaged me an address and the name of the sales lady who could help me. I laughed out loud when I read her name was Brenda.

My angels pointed me in the right direction away from one Brenda toward another. They helped me see that not all Brenda's are bad and that their plan was for my happiness. They assured me that God had a beautiful plan for my new castle of hope.

The next part of my plan involved learning to trust my gut. Each time I dealt with Terry regarding the purchase of my new home, I looked for his snaky manipulation. When he said he was doing me a favor, I listened to hear what he expected in return. There was always an expectation for repayment. He would suggest a blow job for good old times. I told him the good old times were long gone.

I learned to know better than to trust a snake that was unwilling to transform. A snake sheds its skin as it grows. No matter how many skins that snake sheds it will always be a snake. At the core of the snake's symbolism lies the essence of transformation. I transformed my lack of worth to self-confidence. I no longer put myself down or felt inferior to anyone. I walked my own path. I held onto my beliefs and was not swayed by another's. I knew I was being the best possible version of myself, which was as good as anyone else. I expected other snakes to treat me with respect.

My mind returned to the office that I had committed to work in. I knew that my happiness was more important than the administrative role I had agreed to. I accepted that the company I worked for would never be able to pay me my worth.

Before I made the decision to close the book on my past, I needed to make an inventory of the choices I made in my life to get there. I wanted to ensure that I never again chose another's success and happiness over my own. I vowed to end my contract with the pain of co-dependency. I looked at the lies I told myself with honest observation and a kind heart. I saw the reality within each untruth.

The false truth that I was separated from my daughter held me apart from her love. I felt her with my physical body and saw her in my mind. I lived my life with her as I created every project. I talked to her as though she was right beside me. I listened to her wise words. We made a great team.

The false truth that the world was full of scoundrels clouded my vision. The truth was that my angels have aligned me with great allies in business and life. I accepted the truth that Terry was mismanaging the Greystone sale.

I proved that I could make my own fortune. The abundance of wealth in my life was more than the currency in my bank account. Time spent with family and friends was valuable. The worth of each day was measured by the moments treasured. I banked on the fact that my support and expertise had helped people break through the lies that once held them back from realizing their full potential. The hope I offered allowed others to believe that healing was possible.

Each time I met someone where they were at, I offered hope. The place we would venture was uncertain, unknown and dark. The fireflies always came to light our way. Together, we walked to the forest where the monsters live... but they had no power any longer. Each scary tooth fell from their mouth and their roar faded into the silent night. Every step we took brought us closer to the castle of hope we were building together.

View my special message by scanning the code below
OR go to: https://qrco.de/CastleofHope

Chapter 16

Newcastle Way

In 2013, I invested the monies Terry disbursed to me before the sale of the Greystone divorce home and paid the deposit for my new home on Newcastle Way in St. Albert. I felt desperate to escape Greystone. Terry came and went as he pleased after we were divorced. He acted as though he owned the house and me. He would sit beside my bed in the early morning while I slept with a cup of Tim Horton's coffee acting like he was my friend. He would ask me if I still slept naked. I felt unsafe. I was too afraid to change the keys. He told me if I did anything to stop him from coming and going as he pleased, I would be responsible for all the bills. There was no feasible way for me to pay the mortgage, electricity, heating and food bills. I stayed and played the game the way I played the game in our marriage. I kept the peace.

I signed the court ordered transfer Residential Seller Brokerage Agreement to give my consent to the disposition of the Greystone home. I trusted that Terry would fulfill his legal obligation upon sale of the matrimonial home and transfer the court appointed sales proceeds me.

I purchased a home large enough for Chance and me to live in. I chose a house instead of a condo so that our husky-shepherd Mia would have a back yard. The divorce decree was straight forward and exact. Terry was court ordered to pay me a lump sum of money from the sale of the divorce home, spousal and child support. I agreed to the lump sum to avoid any further connection to the spiral of his never-ending loop of chaos. The lump sum agreement did not include any monies from the construction company I had helped build. I did not want to have any connection to possible CRA problems or debt in the future. My intention was to remove myself from his liabilities and move forward away from Terry's secrets and scandals. Sadly, secrets became facts as women came forward to tell me how often he cheated. The same women who he seduced were no longer willing to keep his secrets.

I signed the divorce papers quickly. I wanted to escape the abuse. I needed to get Terry out of my life. He was anxious to have the divorce finalized so that he could marry his fiancée, Brenda. While Terry planned his fairy-tale wedding, I healed emotional wounds and scars that were opened as more truths of his adultery were revealed.

I convinced Jarett, Josh, and Chance to spend Christmas in Kelowna with Terry and his fiancée Brenda. I told them that if their father was going to be spending the rest of his life with her, they needed to stop treating her like the gold-digging other woman. I hoped that if they could develop a relationship with Brenda so that the experience of watching their father remarry would be easier.

I assured them I would be okay spending Christmas alone and could use the time to catch up on some reading. Besides, I had our rescue dogs, Rambo, Duke, and Mia, to keep me company. I kissed the boys goodbye and readied for my first Christmas alone.

I knew that I didn't want to spend every Christmas for the rest of my life without that special someone. I also had to accept the reality that I wasn't a magnetic attraction for Mister Right yet. If I wanted to find a man who would love and accept me for who I was, then I needed to let go of my past, learn to love myself, create a life worth living and release the thoughts that didn't serve me.

I decided that December 23 was the best day to begin the next step on my healing journey. I knew that I would rather spend the rest of my life alone than sacrifice my happiness in order to make a man happy. I sat down in my living room, chose a music playlist, picked a Santa wrapping paper and readied myself to wrap Christmas presents.

I had five crystal necklaces with angel wing pendants that I had bought from Daphne to give to the women I loved. I readied for my new, solo beginning and began to listen to Adele. "Rolling in the Deep" began to play as I cut the first piece of wrapping paper and instantly felt empowered. I knew that I was better off without Terry and knew that the scars on my heart left from his betrayal would eventually heal.

I put my wrapping project aside to dance and celebrate my independence. When the dogs tried to join the dance party, I began to cry. I prayed to my angels to help heal the painful memories in my broken heart. I desperately tried to set fire to the rain that would not stop as years of tears fell from my eyes.

Crying ignited worry about my sons arriving safely in Kelowna. What if I had made a mistake when I encouraged them to travel on the icy roads from Alberta to British Columbia. I began to panic and pace imagining every possible worst-case scenario. I had to stop the hamster wheel in my mind. I picked up the phone, called Tracy and asked if I could come over. I knew I couldn't be alone during the horrendous holiday season.

I fed the dogs and our cat, Chewy, and prepared for an evening cuddled up on Tracy's couch. My silver Navigator carried me to the safety of Jeff and Tracy's second level home.

When I arrived, Tracy wrapped her arms around me and held me as I wept. Her love had been my only safe place. She kept the warrior alive in me every day.

Tracy was the only one who'd confronted Terry about his cocaine addiction because she was not intimidated by his bullying. "Nancy doesn't deserve your shit. You're killing yourself and you need help."

Jeff kept me facing forward and reminded me to wear my crown. He told me, "You deserve better. Don't forget the truth of what he did to you." When I I faltered and believed I was too weak, he encouraged me to continue fighting for the money Terry owed me.

Jeff rolled me a joint and made me dinner. He reminded me that I was always welcome to spend the night on their couch. We spent Christmas Eve watching television, laughing and sharing the greatest gift of all—friendship.

Christmas morning was a special time, and I savored watching them open gifts. Each box was filled with love. When Tracy opened the angel wings I gave her and promised to wear them forever, I cried because forever was never long enough.

After we opened presents, Tracy insisted that I spend Christmas day at Sandra and Bob, her parent's, home. I drove home first to feed the dogs, let them outside, and shower my aching body and soul. Then I called the boys who assured me they'd arrived safely and were making friends with the next Mrs. Chaplin.

I cried after I hung up. I felt bitter, abandoned, betrayed, and hopeless. Why didn't I have a love to come home to? What was the matter with me? I took my rage to the page and journalled until I emptied my heart. Writing helped me share my feelings and gain clarity about what I wanted.

I spent Christmas and boxing day with Tracy's family. I slept on Tracy's couch each night and returned home every morning to take care of the animals, journal and make a plan for the new year. 2015 would be the year that I would create a life that invited more time spent with friends, continued healing, fun with tarot and finding love.

I went for walks with the dogs, practiced yoga, wrote in my journal and slept on Tracy's couch every night until New Year's Eve. I became the third wheel on the love train when I joined Tracy and Jeff at the movies.

Silver Linings Playbook was the love story on the screen that brought me a new understanding of my romantic future—I would have to find someone as crazy as I was who didn't see how fucked-up I had become. After spending a week on Tracy's couch, I needed to be at home to sort through my feelings. I cried myself to sleep that night at home alone, believing I would never find someone to love me.

The next morning, I decided to get crystal clear about what I didn't want. I compared what I didn't want with what I wanted.

Don't Want	Want
Lying	Kind
Cheating	Compassionate
Douche Bag	Hard-working
Cruel Addict	Loyal
Fraud	Funny
Failure	Gentle

Next came the magazines, glue, stickers and paper to solidify the vision of my future. I cut out words that described who I was creating. Pictures of love, laughter, joy and happily-ever-after were cut and glued to create the life I would create.

I thought about all of my failed attempts at love and congratulated myself for being willing to try. Even though online dating had been a disaster, I was willing to try again. One more attempt with the dating world brought me back to an online site with a willingness to find love.

I wanted to find someone with whom to share my time and go to the movies or take a walk in the park. As my fingers typed my profile, Jarett opened the door.

I closed the computer, but his eagle-eyes saw what I'd been doing. He smiled and congratulated me for trying again. We visited for a while and talked about how we spent our time apart. After he left, I finished my profile and activated the account.

View my special message by scanning the code below
OR go to: https://qrco.de/NewcastleWay

Chapter 17

Hey, You...

Dating on the internet was a challenge for me. I looked at the lineup of men on my computer screen and didn't know how to choose Mr. Right so I called my friend, Iva. We were both single, divorced mothers. We met for tea to talk about dating and our children. I picked up the phone and called her to ask if I could come over for a cup of tea.

She opened her door, "What's up with you?" Her eyes sparkled with a knowing smile that something was new.

I admitted to the atrocity of online dating, and she clapped her hands with delight.

Ushering me into the spare room with the computer, she asked me to sign in. She then scooted me—Iva-the-Diva style—out of the chair so she could check out the challengers. She scrolled through a couple profiles and then squealed, "Oh, I like this one!"

"Ugh, no. Not the bald one." I explained my hard *no*, and sighed because she ignored me and kept commenting about how wonderful he was. Instead of arguing, I strolled into the kitchen to pour a glass of wine.

As I savored the red glass of glee, my phone dinged an unusual sound. Looking to see who'd messaged or called, I quickly discovered a green dot above the dating app icon. With a quick click, I saw that someone had liked my profile and sent me a message.

Behind the wall in the spare room, Iva was liking his pictures on my behalf. When I saw what she had done, I was shocked, enraged, confused and frozen in fear.

"What part of I do not want to date a man who has a daughter do you fail to understand?" I asked.

She asked if I was mad. I took a deep breath and checked in with my emotions before responding, "I'm not mad. I'm afraid."

I walked back into the kitchen, took a sip of my wine and a deep breath. Then, I opened the message.

"Hey, you," were the words that brought me the next chapter of love into my life. RC1964 was on my phone! I needed some time to think about what I would do next. I told Iva that I needed to go home to think about how I would handle this situation and decide if I would respond.

When I got home, I asked my angels to help me make the right decision. I sat in the silence and stared at my phone. RC1964 was not the man I'd planned for. Politely, I responded with a, "Hey, you."

We chatted back and forth for several days and got to know each other.

I told him about my dogs and my sons as we planned to meet in person. He told me his name was Ralph and that he was taking care of his daughter's dog Holly.

I brought Mia, my husky shepherd along to sniff him out because she was an excellent judge of character. With a toque, ski pants, a scarf and warm drinks, I exited my SUV at the dog park next to Story Land Valley Zoo. Mia literally dragged me through the snow to the feet of the bald man. He kindly helped me get to my feet and rescued our drinks.

We wandered the snowy paths for hours sharing our stories. Mia sniffed through the snow and jumped through the forest in search of rodents. I began to hope that that maybe he would be worthy of a second date. Never before had I shared my thoughts with someone who I had just met, but I did with him because he had a calm, humble vibe. As our conversation continued, I asked one question, "What's your biggest regret?"

He told me of a property he wished he had purchased—a condo in Belize.

I was shocked because a friend of mine told me about condos in Belize and suggested I buy one. I wondered if it was possible that we had been offered the same opportunity. I was hesitant to share too many details of my life because I still didn't know if Ralph was possibly connected to my past.

I asked my angels to give me courage and asked him if he knew a realtor named Terri Drynan and her boyfriend, Wes. He said yes, she was the friend who had told him about the property.

"Wow! That's incredible. My son Chance and I were in Mexico at her son's wedding last year."

"I used to camp at the same lake as her before my divorce."

We walked back to the parking lot talking about our mutual friend and where we wanted to travel in the future. Ralph helped me get Mia into my SUV and asked if I would like to go out again. I agreed and gave him my cell phone number. I asked if he would text me on my phone instead of the dating app. He agreed.

HEY, YOU...

View my special message by scanning the code below
OR go to: https://qrco.de/HeyYou

Chapter 18

Secrets Revealed

My sons and friends exposed more scandals. I learned of the many prostitutes Terry had been sleeping with after I signed the divorce agreement. I met with one woman who sold her body to feed her children. She introduced me to mothers, daughters and wives who bartered their bodies. I listened to their stories and discovered they all buried the pain and hid the shame.

I remember sitting on the front step of my new home and sobbing wondering why I had been such a fool. Looking back through my memories I saw the limousine rides, lipstick-stained shirt collars and weekend boys' trips with clarity. I had been the loyal, trusting wife who expected my husband to be the same. I had been taught to treat people the way I wanted to be treated. Terry's teachings were different. He demanded respect and was taught to fight for what he wanted. The same skills he learned in the basement of his home when his father taught him how to box were used against me. I wasn't a fool. I was a victim of violence.

I saw Ralph's name on the call display and answered. He asked if I was okay. I said no. He came over immediately and held me as I cried. I fell asleep in his loving arms. I woke up the next morning resting in his embrace and grateful for love in my life. I quietly rolled out of the bed and went into the bathroom.

I struggled to look at myself in the mirror because when I did, I saw a fool who had trusted the man who would not pay eight hundred thousand dollars of the divorce decree. The memories of all the times I had trusted him played in my mind. I shifted my focus with one thought. I can trust. I can believe that the men in my life who love and support me will continue to be loyal, kind, compassionate and trustworthy. I have raised admirable sons and am loved by a wonderful man. I see the promise of a new day.

The love my sons gave me every day was a gift. Their encouragement has helped me stay the course in my healing. Never did they question my need to prioritize self-care. When I studied yoga and became a teacher, they told their friends and encouraged them to come to my classes. The basement in my Newcastle home became my yoga studio. I healed with my students and began to rebuild my shattered confidence.

My sons have grown into wonderful, loyal men. They are caring husbands, wonderful fathers, fabulous uncles and incredible leaders. Despite the example their father gave them as husband and father, they are trustworthy. My sons have created wonderful families. Chance, my youngest son, and his wife Jessy gifted me delightful granddaughters who were blessings. I look into their eyes and see curiosity, tenacity, adoration and faith. I see a reflection of my own eyes.

The inner sight that once haunted my mind and clouded my eyes has changed. Drinking coffee in the morning without wondering if Terry will open the front door without a key is no longer a worry. Midnight calls filled with threats of violence or pleas for me to withdraw the maintenance order no longer wake me. His relentless phone calls can no longer reach me. I have blocked over twenty phone numbers and refuse to answer calls from unknown callers. I no longer listen to him. Thankfully, he has finally stopped calling my phone. My mind was finally at peace and no longer preoccupied with the past.

I no longer argued with his insults and no longer carried the shame of his scandals. I knew that each boat crash, car wreck, failed business and disastrous relationship caused my children to worry. I detached from his continued chaos. I stopped bearing witness to his implosion as he continued to destroy himself.

Instead, I felt saddened by his downfall. I listened every time my sons called to unburden their hearts from a haunted distress call. I practiced unconditional positive regard and stayed silent as they shared every detail of their dilemma. I held space and listened. I knew that if I had nothing nice to say, it was better to say nothing at all.

His miseries were a mixture of high, medium and low mayhem. His lifestyle created chaos and though he intended to change, change was mixed with disorder. One day he was high, and his words were filled with grand schemes to build money-making campgrounds. The next week he was now worrying about how he would be able to pay his bills.

Each promise he made to stop using drugs created hope. I taught my sons to measure his words with wisdom. Accepting what they could not change included their father. Each time he promised to get clean and called high, gave them an opportunity to set a boundary. The line marked the limited area where no trespassers were allowed. Healthy boundaries allowed us to live our lives without suffering from the strains of anxiety, worry and fear about Terry.

I could see the conflict in their eyes when I spoke his name. They were torn about what they told me. I asked them to tell me everything that affected them. I reminded them that unburdening their hearts helped.

I took in all the truths they told me, kept their secrets, hid the scandals and grew increasingly bitter and resentful. My mind was filled with a constant conversation with their father for all the wrong he had done in his life and how it had affected the children. Each morning when I woke, I turned on the coffee maker and settled into writing in my journal. Somedays I wrote about gratitude first and other days I wrote about my frustrations, challenges, obstacles and burdens. The more I emptied my mind onto the page the easier it was to hear the whispers of spirit. My heart longed to heal at a deeper soul level and my angels suggested that I study the ancient healing arts. I knew exactly who I could call to help me.

Tina Lea, my friend in Kelowna, understood my curiosity about the different shamanic practices. I felt safe talking to her because she never judged me and supported me with her loving support after Emily passed. I dialed her number, and she answered on the first ring.

"Oh my God, it happened again. I was just thinking of you and wanted to talk to you about Reiki."

I smiled and told her that I called to talk to her about studying something and that I just didn't know where to start.

"Well, now you do," she giggled.

She explained to me the precepts of reiki and how I could incorporate them into my life. I chose to incorporate a few practices into my daily routine for the next ten days in the morning and at night.

First, I held my hands in prayer, and I spoke these words once in my mind, "For today only, do not anger, do not worry, do your work with appreciation and be kind to all people." Then, I honestly acknowledged how often I became angry, who aggravated me and what circumstances enraged me. When I worried, I looked into the thought to see if I was fretting about someone or something. I noted what memory or situation triggered me. I also paid attention to the work that I enjoyed and when I felt resentment. I carried my journal with me and noted my thoughts, feelings, observations and insight throughout the day.

Next, I began to study the history of Reiki in India, Japan, Hawaii and my own country of Canada. I learned that the universal light force energy could be systematically shared with the human body. I studied the self-healing hand positions that started from the head and moved to the feet. Daily practice allowed me to memorize the routine until I was able to complete the sequence without having to reference pictures from the books I read.

I continued practicing and reading for six months and prayed that my angels would help me find a supportive teacher to learn more from. While I waited, I spent more time at Ralph's home in south Edmonton and occasionally slept over on weekends. It was important to me that I stayed a constant in Chance's life which meant being at my Newcastle home the majority of my time. I maintained a steady balance between working as a bookkeeper, being a good mom, caring for my own mother and trying to become accustomed to being part of a safe, normal relationship with Ralph.

Nightmares interrupted my sleep whether I was at my home or Ralph's. I would wake up crying, sweating, tossing, and turning at least four days a week. The mish mash of dreams was sprinkled with memories of my past painful abuse, abandonment, harm coming to those I loved and images of the bloody dock where I saw Emily's body for the last time. I needed to find a way to move the blocked energy in my body and help me transcend the anxiety that constantly crept into my waking day.

The nervous tension from restless nights and worrisome days had built up in my body and manifested into migraines and bladder infections. I continued working with my therapist, using Bach flower essences, Reiki and regular massages to help me to continue to heal from my C-PTSD (Complex Post Traumatic Stress Disorder).

When Kelly, my massage therapist, told me she was offering a one-on-one weekend Reiki level one workshop, I knew that this was the supportive teacher and safe space I had asked my angels to align me with. Even though I was managing my anxiety, I knew that entering a classroom with other students would add to my angst and interfere with my ability to learn.

I sat in her back yard and enjoyed the blend of Multisensory Teaching Methods which integrated visual, auditory, intuitive and kinesthetic-tactile elements to enhance learning. During the three-day intensive, I received my first series of attunements and became a channel for the limitless source of all love. My life was changed in the most positive way. From the time of the attunement and through the rest of my life, all I needed to do was connect with this love and allow the energy to flow through me.

View my special message by scanning the code below
OR go to: https://qrco.de/SecretRevealed

Chapter 19

No Longer a Victim

I became confident and resourceful. I was no longer a victim of violence. I learned to understand the Battered Women's Syndrome which allowed me to see that there was no wall that stopped me from living my best life. What stopped me from living my best life was fear. I now know that I was brainwashed into believing that I could not leave my marriage.

Again, was the constant in our disfunction. Terry would go on another bender, and I was told it was my fault again. He cried false tears of guilt he'd probably practiced like a politician preparing for the next election. His implication was always the same, "You drive me to drink." He blamed me for his behavior. I did not force him to drink. I learned that I could not force him to change.

I mastered my destiny when I mastered my mind. I studied the psychology of codependency. I countered the always present threat of physical and emotional violence with more honest communication with Tracy. Monthly visits to her nail salon allowed us to spend time together regularly.

I became the queen of my castle when I chose to do what was best for me. Being an only child taught me to be independent. Recovering from being a battered woman taught me to ask for help.

I learned that I needed to continue taking back my power and control. When I took a frank inventory of my life and the choices I had made, I admitted that setting boundaries was a problem for me. If the phone rang, I answered it. I learned to silence my phone and quiet my mind so that I could take better care of myself. Self-care allowed me to focus on what mattered most to me—ME. After I took care of me, I could take care of what needed to be done to support others.

When I supported my aging mom, I used compassion and confidence to help her with her challenges. I visited her often to ensure she was well cared for. Advocating for her disabilities within a health care system that diagnosed the problem and not overall wellness had many challenges.

My mom was often no longer able to understand that transferring to the toilet from her wheelchair without assistance was unsafe. Her memory was no longer clear as it once was. Even though her memory had faded, she still remembered what was important for her happiness.

Wearing panties allowed her to feel liberated. Her self-worth was essential to her cheerfulness. I was happy when my mom smiled and enjoyed the golden years of her life. When she was unhappy, I did what I could to improve her mindset.

With confidence and kickass determination, I ensured that my mom was safely transferred to the toilet. The strong resilient woman who cared for me, was no longer safely able to care for herself. I said no for my mom when no was the best answer for her.

"No, my mother does not need to wear a diaper." My mother wanted to wear panties, and it was the responsibility of the care facility to ensure that staff came when her call button was pushed. When she pushed her call button for transfer assistance, I tracked the time it took for a caregiver to come to her aid. I was patient and knew when to walk to the nurse's station to ask for assistance.

I was kind and direct. "Alice pushed her call button seven minutes ago. She needs immediate assistance to transfer to the toilet from her wheelchair." If more than one nurse was at the station, I kindly spoke to both. "Perhaps one of you lovely ladies can help her. I want to ensure she transfers safely." My stern look commanded attention. My mother required two people to assist her.

I watched and observed as they transferred mom and thanked them with my words and smile. I valued every person who supported my mom. Sadly, I met many obstacles within the government health care system. Shaming seniors is a form of elder abuse. Their fragile bodies and minds need to be cared for with awareness and kindness.

When my mom told me that a nurse made a mean face when she soiled her panties, I felt an anger boiling up inside of me. I checked in with my rage and my memories. Anger and rage separated me from patience and peace. Dissolving feelings of anger and rage by tapping into their subconscious source helped heal my suppressed trauma. Memories offered openings into the past that I could heal in the present.

I remembered when mom joined us for Thanksgiving dinner in the Manor home. She always paid for the turkey and stuffed cash in the diaper bag so that I couldn't argue about paying. This time she saw the card for the Edmonton Women's Shelter that Tracy had left in the side zipper pocket. She left a note with one word, "Emergency" and two one-hundred-dollar bills.

My rage wasn't from the memory of the note. My repressed anger came from the memory of how often Terry bought loyalty from his family with money. I always felt like his family took his side in the divorce because of the lavish loans and generous gifts he gave them. He would fill birthday cards with ten or twenty hundred-dollar bills for his nieces, nephews, mom and sister.

My mom's loyalty was always for me. She lent me the money I needed to continue my education and always asked how my studies were going. I do not remember what courses I completed between Introduction to Psychology and Abnormal Psychology. I do remember the words my professor kindly wrote on front page, right corner of my endeavor:

Creative writing would better suit your success.

Next to these wise words was a large red *zero*. I could either accept the zero and begin creative writing courses or fight the zero and appeal my mark. I picked up my journal and began to write. I wrote about the future I wanted to create and the changes I needed to make in my life.

I described the peaceful home I deserved to live in. I glued pictures of happy families and fun adventures into my journal. I drew smiley faces, peace signs, hearts and butterflies. I detailed the choices that took away from my happiness. Saying I was fine when I was sad was unhealthy. Pretending I was happy when I was enraged created misery. Focusing on Terry's wellness while neglecting my own health damaged my body, mind and soul.

Writing became a priority. Trying to change Terry became unimportant. Ahead of me were ten more years of unhappiness if I was willing to wait for Emily to graduate before I left my marriage. My daughter adored her father. Terry often gave her a few fifty or hundred-dollar bills so she could buy whatever she wanted. He made up for his absences with money and bought her adoration. Leaving him meant my children would have less time with one parent. Creating a life without him was filled with uncertainty and certainty. Doubt stopped me from doing anything. Prayer and meditation helped me focus on the wonderful possibilities and endless opportunities that could be. I was certain that I was imaginative and able to create a happier, more peaceful home.

Reading and writing fed my imagination and helped me create a better reality while I learned to coexist with the beast I married. Emily and I giggled beneath blankets as we read late into the evenings. Story time became our nightly ritual as we shared my love of language. We imagined our castle and planned for a life where peace and happiness filled our new home. Beauty would leave the beast and live happily ever after.

On weekends we walked in the neighborhoods, and I wrote down phone numbers for real estate agents. I took small actions every day to plan for my future without Terry.

I watched him party with the boys and cared less if he strayed. His loyalty mattered less; my happiness mattered more. I planned my future without him. I was sure that if he was truly cheating on me, someone would tell me.

Somewhere between Emily's first and fifth years of school, her father found his mistress. Not the woman he later married, but the whore who carried a disease. I don't know if she knew she was contagious; perhaps she was too tired to care or too coked out to know. Maybe Fat Daddy Chap kept her in a lie like he had with me with his, "One day, I'll rescue you" routine. His charm and charisma created a wonderful smokescreen hiding the fact that his rap sheet is a frightening list of crimes committed over the span of forty years.

First, the bait, "Hey beautiful do you want to go for a boat ride?" The lure includes a rose, a box of chocolates, free booze, pre-rolled joints and a party boat full of fun people.

Second the hook, "I wish I could spend the entire day with you; but I need to go home to my wife who has cancer."

The pretty fish then swallows the hook, "Oh, you're such good husband."

Followed by his, "One day I'll leave her and be with you babe."

Breaking free from his chaos allowed me to see that what he called "crazy whack-job" suspicions were more fact that fiction. I recognized that the activation of anger in my mom's room with the nurse was rooted in suppressed trauma. I smiled at the memory that no longer had power over my choice to be patient and peaceful.

I returned to the present moment with mom and asked her to press her call button to call a nurse. When the nurse arrived, I asked mom, "Is this the lady who helped you with your soiled panties?" She shook her head and said she couldn't remember. I assured her all the nurses would be made aware of the importance of treating all patients with dignity and respect. I spoke to mom's case manager who spoke to the wellness team. I was assured that the staff would be educated on the importance of emotional wellness.

Walls are built to protect. Harmful intruders are kept on the outside. Love inside the walls allows us to feel safe. When the people who vow to keep us safe cause us harm, changes must be made.

View my special message by scanning the code below
OR go to: https://qrco.de/NoLongerAVictim

Chapter 20

Lemon Drops

My daughter's laughter and snuggles comforted me during the lonely nights when her daddy didn't come home. I never complained when she asked if we could have a sleepover in my bed. I filled one big bowl with popcorn and promised we would stay up late and watch movies. We took turns picking films and loved stories with happy endings. Often, we read the book before the movie and sometimes the reverse.

I learned to live a life of joy from the lessons she taught me before and after her death. Life with Emily was filled with silly songs, funny skits, hip hop dances and laughter. She loved fun breaks and believed they were more important than adult stuff which she insisted was stupid. "Why clean the floor so much mum, we don't eat off it."

She preferred fun floor washing which was having a bath and laying her soaking wet towel down on the hallway floor then scooting while singing, "I'm a moppidy mop, boppidy bop." Then, she would flip over onto her back and sing, "If all the raindrops were lemon drops and gumdrops, oh what a rain that would be. I'd stand outside with my mouth open wide. Ah, ah, ah, ah, ah, ah, ah, ah, ah, ah." She warned me that, "All work and no play will make you an old witch." Her infectious giggle as she imitated an old lady walking with a cane helped me remember that fun was more important than a clean home.

When she died, our home became a hollow empty coffin. The sour taste of injustice was a struggle for me. The red solo cups that littered the boat that hit the Sea-doo were proof to me that someone was drinking the day that Emily died. We never had an opportunity to prove that the boat driver wasn't drinking. Blood samples were only taken from my son to test his blood alcohol levels while he lay in the hospital battered and broken. The police didn't deem it necessary to test the boat driver.

I held onto the anger until I learned to unburden my heart. Studying Reiki allowed me to free myself of fury and live in peace. When I placed my hands on the lowest part of my belly to send energy to my root chakra, I saw Emily dancing in her sparkly red dress in the kitchen practicing her hip-hop routine. As the memories flooded my mind, I allowed the tears to flow. The blood-red rage softened each day that I practiced self-reiki. Twenty-eight days of focused healing taught me that my energy mattered. I learned that I must fill my body with light energy to be able to love and support others.

After reiki, I boldly healed from every fear that I had about my living children. I learned that it was natural to fear for the lives of my other children. The loss of one child had me fearing for the loss of my other children. What I feared more than the death of my remaining children, was my own. I did not want my children to suffer the pain of losing a sister and a mother.

I faced my death by writing a will. Then, I learned how to support others by studying to become an End-of-Life Doula. I saw the pain that bitterness added to death. Hostile emotions within a family when death nears increased the pain their loved one was already suffering. Offering compassionate support to my clients allowed them to die with more ease. Hearing the near dead tell me about their vision of the afterlife they saw was beautiful. Holding the hand of the dying is a blessing that I was honored to share.

When I needed to unburden my heart after supporting a client, I walked in the forest. Death taught me to accept what I cannot change and to see the beauty in all life. When I strolled in the forest and talked with angels, Emily walked beside me. I saw the beauty of her in each walking stick I held. I smiled and sighed knowing that all work and no play created crankiness in me. Hearing her angelic voice from the other side of life helped me let go of the challenges in my day.

Sometimes when the sky was dark, I saw the beauty of the northern lights. I felt their energy when I stood beneath their brilliance. Each time I experienced magnificence, I felt even more connected to Emily. The song that I chose as her song for the celebration of life *"If I Die Young"* by The Band Perry sung in my mind. I knew that love never, ever dies and she was shining her love down on me as I stood under the purple and green colors.

When I over cared for others and neglected my self-care, I talked to Jarett. He was my lifeline to a supportive voice who listened and loved unconditionally. He understood my triggers because we both suffered from abuse and codependency within the same family unit. I was able to be honest with him. I did not scuffle with drugs or alcohol. I wrestled with patterns like people pleasing and meticulousness.

Recovery was important to me. I knew that appeasement was a symptom of greater dis-ease. The self-defeating belief that I needed to make others happy to be happy was destructive. I recognized that the root of my self-destructive behavior was years of trying to make my ex-husband happy. The false belief was that if he was happy, he would stay home with his family and be the husband that I wanted him to be. The realization that I could not change him allowed for a life where I focused on changing myself.

I went to co-dependents anonymous—CODA meetings—to help me understand how abuse, addiction, gambling, adultery and financial stress contributed to my codependency. I learned, I listened, I changed.

Now, I prefer listening to the birds and sipping a glass of iced tea. I keep my optimism level high by celebrating my success at the end of each day. If pessimistic thoughts enter my mind, I remind myself that imperfect actions lead to optimal success.

Jarett works with metal. He cuts and bends sheets, his trade is a sheet metal worker. He is a tin artist because he infuses heart into every project he creates. After a strenuous day, he goes to the beach. Water helps him heal from the pain in his hands and the hurt that he still holds in his heart from Emily's death. Even though I have told him time and time again that her death was not his fault, guilt still plagues his heart. Being a mom means holding space in my heart for him to heal. I do this by healing myself.

View my special message by scanning the code below
OR go to: https://qrco.de/LemonDrops

Chapter 21

Less Faith ...
Not Faithless

One of the biggest misconceptions I have encountered as a psychic medium is about my spiritual beliefs. When I was asked a question by a client who had lost a child, I wasn't shocked. I needed to take a sip of tea before I answered.

"Did someone hurt you to make you lose your faith, or is that something you'd rather keep hidden?"

I lost my faith in Jesus and the church long before I developed my gifts of clairaudience and clairvoyance. The truth is, these gifts brought me to a place of living in the light of Christ's consciousness more than any formal religious practice ever did in my years of being a Christian. I lost my faith in Jesus the day my daughter's body and soul were returned to heaven without me.

I didn't simply lose my faith; I developed a deep, loathing, and vicious hatred for both the Son and the Father. My hatred went far beyond any mortal man or woman. My hatred went beyond any pain I suffered at the hands of man and woman. I directed my wrath at the man who I had trusted to protect me, the man I had trusted to protect us both.

How could I ever love him when he had stolen her from me like a thief in the night? He had her blood on his hands. I hated him and I turned away from him in disgust and despise. When I called to him in the night, he abandoned me. Then he took the only belonging on the earth that I loved more than life itself—my child. Then he charged my son with her death. I hated him so much that I hoped he would suffer the eternal damnation I was left to suffer here in my own hell.

I'll try to explain how my hatred happened. Jesus didn't take my daughter from me; the man who I believe drove the boat—Richie Rich—robbed me of more time with Emily. His carelessness changed our lives forever.

I wonder if he will ever contact me or my son. Will he take a step further than the card he wrote carefully with his lawyer? He avoided litigation. Perhaps he has found salvation.

The promise of eternal life with my daughter helped me learn to practice forgiveness. I have pardoned Terry for many offenses and wrongdoings. I let go of my resentment and desire for revenge because I wanted to be more compassionate. Yet, I couldn't help but wonder if he knew the damage he caused by accusing Jarett of killing his baby sister.

I know that I will never be able to have a conscious conversation with him about that day. His choice to destroyed himself with drugs was a series of self-defeating patterns that moved him far away from active listening, presence, awareness and non-judgement. The disease of addiction is his affliction. He is tormented.

Living in faith became easier for me when I began to trust in the love of the men who loved me. I opened my heart to healing and shared my psychic gifts with those who were willing to listen.

View my special message by scanning the code below
OR go to: https://qrco.de/LessFaithNotFaithless

Chapter 22

Sedona Arizona

Terry loved to tell people he could sell ice cream to an Eskimo. He was proud of his sales skills and didn't see the connection between integrity, honesty, quality, commitment and customer satisfaction. He was willing to bend or break rules, cheat, or engage in unethical behavior to secure a win. I saw the tragic effects of addictive and chaotic behaviors wreak havoc on his relationships within business, friendships and family.

In 2015, I continued to step further away from the chaos of his life. Each day brought opportunities for self-awareness and clarity. I looked more closely at my own self-sabotaging behavior. I saw how often I allowed myself to be treated with disrespect in the workplace.

Climbing the corporate ladder meant taking on more responsibility. I stepped up with ease as I created systems to track sales and monitor marketing success. Spreadsheets were my specialty, and I was able to merge data from one program into another to create presentations that wooed the owner of the oil and gas company I worked for.

The problem was that the more I did the more I was expected to do. I was sent to corporate headquarters in Arizona, treated like a princess, given more responsibility and set up to fail. When I was tasked to create the marketing plan, I took all my creative skills and developed a PowerPoint presentation with fabulous statistical data. The problem was that I needed to include a budget to finalize the plan, and the owner refused.

For six weeks I struggled with the daily emails from corporate head office asking where the overdue marketing plan was. I replied to every email and copied the owner of the company to ensure that everyone involved knew that I was doing my best. Covering your ass in corporate is important to ensure that you don't get hung out to dry, thrown under the bus, screwed over and blamed for the inadequacy of another.

I also decided that I was no longer willing to put more skin in the corporate game. The no pain, no gain and working your butt off for a paycheck while sacrificing your own wellness game was no longer my happy place. I knew that there was more to life than financial success at the cost of my health and happiness.

I wrote my resignation letter, gave six weeks' notice, booked my flight, found accommodations and committed to a six-day SRT intensive in Sedona Arizona. The benefits of Spiritual Response Therapy had helped me remove the blocks that prevented me from accepting my ex-sister-in-law Leslie's relationship with Terry's new wife Brenda. I wanted to learn to process and share the benefits with my friends and family.

I trained Sally, the order desk manager, to manage the spreadsheet system I had developed and left the company feeling fabulous. The hours we shared during her training helped us get to know each other. We promised to stay friends and kept in touch.

I packed my blanket, journal, courage and faith to help me on my first solo adventure. Travelling alone was an experience that brought me both excitement and terror. I was motivated to learn SRT and filled with anxiety because I was afraid that

Ralph would leave me while I was gone. Facing the false fear meant embracing the feeling by courageously writing my truth. I knew that I would feel better cuddling up in my blanket with my journal and sharing my doubt.

Ralph drove me to the airport, carried my suitcase to the check-in counter, kissed me goodbye and assured me everything was going to be okay. I trusted his love and knew that facing my fear of abandonment would help us grow stronger together.

When the plane took off, I trusted that the big metal masterpiece would fly. I thought of the pilot and crew who ensured that our flight was a success. I was confident that my luggage was stored in the cargo bay beneath me.

After the fasten seatbelt light turned off, I went to the bathroom and laughed as I flushed the toilet because I knew that the waste was cared for and I didn't have to do anything. So often I drained my energy worrying about what was beyond my control. Remembering that focusing on my feelings gave me an opportunity to channel my focus into the present moment and concentrate on the beauty of the now moment.

As soon as I sat down, the man next to be began to snore and I laughed at the beauty of the moment. I was grateful that I wouldn't have to engage in idle chit chat with a stranger. The opportunity to journal about my doubt and reframe my thoughts allowed me to set the stage for success.

I reflected on past experiences and outcomes that triggered my doubt. I took an honest inventory of the skeletons in my closet. I wrote my secrets and past actions that I keep hidden because they were embarrassing, shameful, and potentially damaging if revealed. I knew they were causing stress and anxiety, straining relationships and could prompt reputational damage.

I wrote about being afraid that my hidden addiction could become public knowledge. I admitted that I was worried that my mom would find out that I had not become the lady she expected. I asked my angels to help transmute my shame and help me connect with a supportive environment where I felt safe to disclose past mistakes. With peace in my mind and hope in my heart, I closed my eyes and allowed myself to rest.

I woke when the plane began its descent into Flagstaff, Arizona. I interlaced my fingers and stretched my arms above my head and turned my head from side to side. Keeping my eyes closed allowed me to focus on my breath which helped me slowly connect to the outside world. After a few breaths, I opened my eyes and immediately noticed that my journal was not in my lap.

"Excuse me miss," said the voice to my right. I turned to see the smiling stranger next to me, was holding my journal, pen, cell phone and purse.

"You dropped these while you were snoring," he chuckled. "My wife always says I snore like a freight train. Now, I understand what she means."

"Oh my, I'm so sorry. I didn't mean to disturb you," I replied.

"It's okay you only snored for a few minutes."

I laughed and thanked him for kindly picking up my belongings.

The Universe had shown me with incredible immediacy how supportive it was through the kindness of a stranger. Knowing that I was loved and cared for helped me move forward toward my next step of uncertainty.

After the plane landed, I collected my luggage and flagged town a taxi to take me to Sedona. I gave the driver the address and messaged Susan Carollo, my teacher, to let her know that I had arrived safely, and I was enroute to her home.

Six weeks earlier when I enrolled in the SRT training program, Susan invited me to share a room in her home. I accepted her offer and thanked my angels for helping me find affordable accommodations.

As I sat in the taxi, I thought of all of the magical ways that the puzzle pieces came together. When I trusted in the universe and leapt forward in the direction of my dreams, I manifested beautiful connections.

The art of Spiritual Response Therapy allowed me to open the Akashic Records and identify, clear, resolve and transcend blocked energies. SRT training opened my heart and mind to a level of understanding far beyond anything I had ever imagined in my wildest dreams.

Learning SRT was an integral part of my recovery from co-dependency. I knew that I needed a process to continue to dissolve the block of self-preservation. Deep within my heart wall were more traumas that were destined to open for healing.

I discovered that the betrayals I had experienced taught me to choose my tribe with care. Meeting kind, compassionate students at the retreat helped me see that there were many people who served as guides on my journey. Understanding that even the most horrendous villains were my teachers allowed me to forgive.

Knowing how my subconscious mind had protected me gave me a deeper understanding of my own psychology. The years of my university studies became much more valuable to me because I was able to see the connection to my soul contracts.

I saw who the souls were who incarnated with me for a second round of studies. Gratitude filled my heart when I understood that every villain came to teach me a lesson.

View my special message by scanning the code below
OR go to: https://qrco.de/SedonaArizona

Chapter 23

Walls of Protection

I tattooed each healing accomplishment on my body and created a showpiece that illustrated my story of success. Radical change became my mission as I exposed each trapped emotion that had constructed a wall around my heart. Trapped emotions became a part of my reality because I was unable to heal from the traumas in my life when they happened. Surviving trauma meant stuffing messy emotions away until I was able to deal with them. Fugly emotions like grief, resentment, worthlessness, inadequacy, insecurity, aggression and hatred were saved until I had the necessary time, energy, space and resources to deal with them. "Fugly" is a compound word and slang term derived from combining the words "f***ing" and "ugly."

Each day I avoided healing, I added another rock to my suitcase full of pain. I carried my baggage with me and was not able to give pure love because the love energy that was in my heart could not give freely. I focused on the pain, thought more about my past than my present and grew weary.

My suitcase full of misery was a burden that prevented me from receiving the love that was being radiated toward me by other people. My resentments and bitter betrayals created layers of protection that blocked love from fully entering my heart. I was going through my life partially insulated from others because of the emotional traumas I had been through and the subconscious wall that literally existed around my heart. The traumas I endured were genuine and there was no doubt that they caused more pain than my body thought it could stand to feel again. My body created an energetic wall around my heart one layer at a time.

When I asked Spirit to help me understand the composition of my heart wall, they showed me steel, copper, concrete and diamonds. Steel was used to protect me from direct hits, copper was used for deflection, concrete acted as a fire barrier and diamonds were used to ward off evil.

I saw the purpose of the wall of protection and knew that it was time to remove the layers to allow me to connect with the people I loved most. I knew the importance of clearing the trapped trauma and healing my heart wall. I prioritized my own healing and felt the results the incredibly profound SRT offered as I identified, cleared and removed the blocks to accepting healing. I regained my serenity and began to once again feel connected to the people around me. Once again, I felt God's love for me.

I stayed connected to love each day by practicing meditation in the morning. Meditation helped me tune into where my emotional set point was. I aimed for courage because I knew that it was the power energy I needed to create change in my life. Being willing to try new things and deal with the ebb and flow of life moved me forward in the direction of my dreams. If my energy was in the lower energy vibrations of shame, guilt, apathy, grief and fear, I asked my angels to help me acknowledge that I was worthy of healing. They helped me understand that we are all healers because we are Spirit. This meant that I was a Light Being that had inhabited a physical body. Being filled with light meant that I had unlimited potential. With this infinite possibility, I could learn how to heal each heart wound.

As I continued to experience life, I allowed my daily life experiences to show me where I was still skeptical, terrified, insecure, hostile and remorseful. I honestly inventoried my experiences each day as I continued to journal my journey. Each day I wrote, Spirit helped me revealed more trapped emotions. I released layers of hurt by acknowledging the trauma I had experienced since childhood. I used my pendulum and the SRT system to dissolve blocks to my success and positive expression.

Each day I dedicated myself to healing, helped me feel confident, liberated, loving, playful and sensitive again. I became more able to give and receive love freely. The greater I healed, the more I experienced very interesting and wonderful happenings.

This was how I was meant to live. I was meant to live vibrancy, health, love and joy. Love in its purest form has the highest vibration. The more I healed my heart the greater I was able to generate and receive love. My passion for healing became a part of my every day as I began to share SRT, journalling, meditation and the power of prayer with family, friends and my ever-increasing list of clients.

Sharing my healing gifts became more important to me. I was eager to attract more customers and decided to network to increase my potential customer base. Connection became increasingly important to me as I excitedly entered many different communities of entrepreneurs and leaders in commerce.

My tattoos offered a wonderful opportunity for conversation because I loved to observe other people's artwork. If you want to get to know somebody, ask them about their tattoos. It is really a remarkable way to get to know them. Ask them about their tattoo artists. They will tell you the tale of people that etched their bodies. You may have the opportunity to learn about their best and worst experiences in the world of tattoos.

I loved telling the tale of the tattoo on my back because it allowed me to share my belief that mistakes are opportunities. My very special ink is a replication of the cover from the Tao of Pooh, one of my most favorite books. Beneath the artwork is the old Pooh, the classic Pooh. This is a tattoo that I received from a man training to become a tattoo artist. I could have called his attempt a mistake and shamed myself for the choice. Instead, I saved the memory and learned to choose my next tattooist after careful research.

The stories that people have shared with me about their tattoos tell of battles fought, won and sometimes lost. I love hearing of the hero who has etched their skin with ink. I listen to the tale of the fool and the journey. Fools are warriors dedicated to winning. Fools are dreamers who are willing to chance losing.

We all have different ways of recovering from the pain of loss. Some of us heal from heartache with meditation and others stick needles in their veins filled with heroin. These are obviously two different paths that are seemingly not directly related. I could have chosen heroin. Instead, I chose meditation. I'm grateful I did.

I knew that if chose to avoid the pain with alcohol, drugs, shopping, working out, working a job, or any other way of avoiding it, I would continue to suffer. Trying to avoid pain would be like trying to avoid death—neither were possible! What I decided to do was to choose living heaven here on earth. Creating a life worth living and a legacy to be proud of would make this spin around the sun special. I continued to focus on healing and constructing an amazing life.

View my special message by scanning the code below
OR go to: https://qrco.de/WallsOfProtection

Chapter 24

Relapse or Restoration

Blessings didn't always come wrapped in beautiful packages. Sometimes, they came buried beneath disappointment. I didn't see the sparkle of promise; I only felt the stab of pain.

During the plane ride home, I envisioned how I would share SRT with my family and friends. With my eyes closed and my heart opened, I saw the unlimited potential that this incredible healing modality offered.

I have learned many lessons in my battle through recovery from co-dependency because I stayed the course. I continued to build a better life each day by acknowledging my oopsie daisy mistakes, accepting that I cannot change the past and bravely staying determined to my goals.

My excessive need to be liked and accepted was a symptom of codependency. I often went to great lengths to please others at my own expense which made me an exceptional administrator, great friend, super mom and spectacular wife. It also created another layer in my multi-level addiction journey because I over gave, worked myself into exhaustion, donated too much of my time and tried to solve problems before they happened.

One of my favorite learned lessons is OCD—One Common Denominator. All of my life experiences, including both my failures and successes, are because of my input and output. When I have a positive mindset, I create great, wonderful, amazing and joyful experiences. If I think negative, pessimistic, doubtful and self-sabotaging thoughts, I am part of the evolution of my negative experiences. I am able to create great experiences in my every day because I know that all change is possible. I begin with me. I allow others to do the same.

I also have learned to surrender my other OCD affliction— Obsessive Compulsive Dialogue. I no longer expect myself to have all the answers. I resigned my self-appointed post as Master of the Universe. I allow the Great Creator of All to rise the sun, set the moon, hold the stars and care for all that I cannot care for while caring for myself.

When I fell back into this self-proclaimed status and began practicing excessive caregiving and worrying, I experienced a negative impact on my own well-being. Relapsing into self-destructive patterns happened quickly if I wasn't keenly protective of my wellness. I could convince myself that I deserved calorie and chemical rich treats like chips, candies, ice cream and deep-fried foods instead of choosing self-care that supported my recovery. The next day, I would fall deeper into the negative spiral because I felt guilty.

I'm so grateful to have had the chance to experience this position. I know the skills I've learned over the past forty-eight years will serve me well in my new role. It is with great joy I acknowledge and accept my true position as a Healer of Hearts and Practitioner of Patience and Peace.

I fought my demons for a long time. Longer than many of you have known me. I did not abandon them; I did not give them tough love like many told me to. I continued to go to Al-Anon and Co-Anon meetings and listened to my fears. I did the steps for years because I walked in the shoes of addiction, and I have walked beside an addict. I became a codependent. I learned about boundaries and implemented my own. I did not kick my addict to the curb, professing tough love, either. I loved my addicts, and they know who they are. I do not need to publicly list them nor would I. Never will I give up on them.

I honor my boundaries and theirs. I ask that they do the same. With mutual love and respect, we can both heal. I live by example. Both success and failure I openly share. I am equally proud of both. I will always love me, and I will always love my addicts.

After I divorced Tery and dug deep into my patterns of addiction, I struggled with nasty nightmares—cling-on dreams, the kind I keep falling back asleep no matter what I did to shake them. I also had perfect nights of sleep—gentle, peaceful, and restful. The kind that makes me smile when I wake up. Nightmares and sweet dreams. Darkness and light. The only way I could escape the nightmare was to turn on the light. It's that way in life, too.

The stress of our lives can cause us such incredible pain and agony. The mental anguish of the trauma manifests into physical pain. It's our warning system. The beautiful highways in our body and mind—the miracle highways. Our engine is miraculously filled with fuel and the highways are paved with gold when we are born.

When your sleep is restless, take time to reflect about the stressors in your life. I did and I am. Make change in your life where you can. Accept what you can't. Be wise enough to know the difference.

RELAPSE OR RESTORATION

View my special message by scanning the code below
OR go to: https://qrco.de/RelapseOrRestoration

Chapter 25

Blocks and Bach

December 22, 2015, the divorce home sold for $850,000.00. Terry paid me $72,280.00, used the balance to pay off the mortgage and promised to pay me the outstanding court appointed debt he owed me in lump sum payments.

I stayed the course in my promise to continue to heal myself and work through how to forgive myself for being married to a man who continued to spend recklessly with his new wife. My therapist recommended a few books to guide me through unburdening my angry heart when Terry demanded that I pay for the hot tub that I moved from Greystone to Newcastle.

His "it's only fair," justification made me laugh because I found the funny in the fact that I bought the physical property where he told me he loved me but wasn't in love with me. While he vacationed in Mexico, I obtained the real property report and building permits to allow for additional funds to be released from the lawyer that were held in trust. I reframed the mounting frustration that I felt by seeing each obstacle I jumped over as an opportunity to get the money I deserved.

I focused my energy on dissolving the walls that had been built around my heart for protection. My vow to never let another man hurt me blocked me from living my best life. The oath prevented me from fully accepting love from Ralph and my sons.

This was the day that I would once again connect with my spirit guides and allow their wisdom to guide me. I picked up my pendulum and began the process of opening my Akashic Records. When the storehouse doors opened, I identified the blocks that prevented me from allowing myself to be loved.

Low self-esteem, appeasement, injustice and lying were the discordant energies that blocked my happiness. I cleared any vows made at any time for any reason and replaced them with free will. I trusted my high council and the process of SRT Spiritual Response Therapy and chose a different vow to amplify my wellness.

I pledged that I would open my soul to healing and allow myself the gift of self-care every day for one month. Fifteen reiki hand positions were practiced three times a day for thirty-one days. Journalling followed each session, and a nap was included every afternoon.

My life changed dramatically, and I was able to remove the shackles that I had been fighting to break free from for over twenty-five years. I realized that fear and anxiety were preventing me from allowing myself to be loved. I continued to use Bach flower essences to support my emotional health and allow myself to tap into my fears. Naming my fears allowed me to audit my mindset daily.

Mimulus was the flower essence that helped me face the known fear that Terry may never pay me the money he owned me. It also helped me recognize that I was afraid to fully dive into a career as an energy healer. Adding the flower essence Scleranthus to my Bach blend helped me remedy my indecision and choose to enroll in level two reiki.

I focused on my new life while Terry purchased a penthouse in Mexico with nis new wife Brenda. Together they also built homes in Kelowna and Sylvan Lake. It was a challenge to buy into his story that he couldn't pay me the divorce money still owed. When they acquired a Regal 35 Sport Coupe yacht and a Mercedes-Benz, I discharged my rage with more energy healing.

Every time a post popped up on social media detailing their rockstar lifestyle, I scrolled past. Even though the smell of Terry's lies was putrid, I was able to focus on what mattered most in my life. Creating a life with lasting happiness, fulfillment and success was my focus.

Terry ignored my text messages and when I called, he refused to answer. When he finally returned my voice mail messages, he complained that I was harassing him and upsetting Brenda. He warned me, "Keep fucking around and you'll find out who I'll send to shut your toilet."

I was less intimidated by his fury. I acted immediately and called my lawyer. He suggested that I record all future phone conversations.

I moved through the uncertainty and aggravation with ease because I stayed the course with Bach and self-reiki. I focused on my mental wellness and spiritual health to help me create a life with more joy.

I was curious and had a thirst for more knowledge about the energetic body. I furthered my education and attuned as a Reiki II Practitioner. I jumped in with two hands and feet and enjoyed sharing with my friends. It was a great hobby, and I had fun.

I dedicated the next year to obtaining my third-degree certification. Sharing the gift of reiki with family and friends allowed me to share the gift of energy healing. Each person had different energy blocks, emotional struggles, physical discomforts and reasons for choosing to try energy work.

Studying the first degree taught me to feel within myself where energy was blocked or lacking. The second degree, practitioner, allowed me to share the art of energy balancing with friends and family. The third degree, master, was about making a commitment, for life, to the reiki healing practice and spiritual discipline.

Choosing to be a master was the decision to live peace, serenity, gratitude, integrity, kindness and grace. The choice was a sacred responsibility that required not only knowledge and experience, but also wisdom, understanding, compassion and a genuine interest in people.

I was glad to have chosen the calling. I had yet to see how valuable my reiki practice would be as I dealt with the difficult years that were coming.

View my special message by scanning the code below
OR go to: https://qrco.de/BlocksAndBach

Chapter 26

Sacred Hearts Sisterhood

I closed my eyes, crossed my fingers, trusted Daphne and joined the Sacred Hearts Sisterhood in the spring of 2018. Betrayal had left me feeling uncertain about women and their intentions. Even though I had girlfriends who were loving and supportive, I struggled to know how to identify the villains.

When Daphne suggested I take a leap of faith and write a chapter for *Finding Your Wings*, the second book in the Sacred Hearts series, I said no. Choosing to take the pen in my hand and write for publication was not calculated into my five-year plan.

Daphne encouraged me to embrace my discomfort and reclaim my wild, happy, healthy self. She knew that I loved journalling and told me that I had a great talent for writing. "Great gifts are meant to be shared," she reminded me with a wink and a smile.

After a few weeks, I delighted her with a phone call, and agreed to write a chapter. Within a few hours I received an email from the series creator. My first thought was, "What the fuck is Brenda contacting me for!" Then, belly laughs and understanding.

Spirit had led me to work with a different reflection of the Brenda character in my story. Knowing that the creator of all life loved me allowed me to trust that this opportunity was for my greater good. I understood that I needed to allow another lady with the same name into my life. I accepted the opportunity. I knew that our connection would help me see my authentic power, fine tune my writing skills, connect me with wonderful friends and teach me to be more compassionate.

I learned the power was forgiveness. Writing my chapter came easily, editing brought greater clarity, finding new friends gave me great joy and publishing allowed me to share my experience.

I learned that there was a Better Brenda who would listen to me and support my growth. I discovered that not all women were in my life to cause me harm. I made new friends, created future opportunities for collaboration and accepted that I had deeper pain to heal.

Sharing my story in *Sacred Hearts Rising: Finding Your Wings* gave me the opportunity to write about my drug addiction publicly. Telling my truth helped me soften my shame. I still felt humiliated and angry with Terry's blatant disregard for me and his defiance of our payment agreement.

I took the next crucial step and called my friend Theresa who was a hypnotherapist and reiki master. She had helped me access the trapped memories in my mind that were at the core of my self-sabotaging behavior. Accessing my subconscious blocks had helped me overcome my hyper vigilant cleaning disorder when I was still living in Greystone. I discovered that my fear came from an experience at the age of three when Auntie Eileen screamed at my cousins for not keeping their rooms clean. Learning to reframe the experience allowed me to transform my life and allow myself to go outside and play even if the housework wasn't done.

I trusted that if she could help me access the trapped memories from my childhood then, together we would find the key to overcome the shame and humiliation I was struggling with.

My second session with Theresa helped me see my life from the eyes of an eagle. I saw the people in my life as characters in a story. The entire journey of my life was structured for my growth and healing. Each person played a pivotal role, and I had the freedom of choice in every encounter.

My psychic abilities blossomed as I healed. Each time the dead spoke to me asking me to connect with their loved ones, I felt more aligned with my purpose. I began to see spirit every day and enjoyed sharing messages with people about what the angels shared with me.

View my special message by scanning the code below
OR go to: https://qrco.de/SacredHeartsSisterhood

Chapter 27

2020 Vision

In February of 2020, when Ralph and I entered the airport for our two-week trip to Puerto Vallarta, my life changed. As we waited in line to check our luggage in, I began to notice that some people were wearing yellow badges on their clothes. Golden stars in a circle exactly like the pentacle shape on a tarot card shone around me.

I asked Ralph if he saw them. He looked around, shook his hand, smiled and told me, "No babe. It's just you."

I knew that what I was seeing was a message from beyond the veil. I trusted that I would receive more information. Having patience was easier for me when I trusted that my guides would tell me more soon.

We checked in our baggage and proceeded to the customs area. Ralph chatted with the security agent and teased me for carrying my pillow, blanket, books and the kitchen sink in my backpack. Funny guy loved to joke with strangers and often made friends on the plane.

Travelling with Ralph was always an adventure. His jovial, friendly personality attracted a crowd full of people. We were the perfect blend of introvert and extrovert. I looked for intimate conversations and he just wanted to "shoot the shit."

After completing our Canada Customs inspection, we walked to the restaurant for breakfast. Our tradition was to have a cocktail to celebrate the beginning of our next adventure. I was looking forward to a break from the chaos of my administrative career.

As I sat waiting for my meal, I watched the travelers and their spirit friends walk by. I had become accustomed to seeing what others did not see as my psychic gifts amplified. Music often played in my ears, movies played in my mind's eye, dead people communicated with me during readings and spirit spoke through me daily. I embraced my talents and practiced my craft through mediumship, energy clearing, coaching and writing.

Life was good. I began to feel like my world had finally changed for the good. I was filled with optimism and positive expectation.

Feeling safe in my relationship with Ralph allowed me to talk openly about spirit, angels, death, transformation and manifestation. The more I shared the greater I felt. For the first time in my life I was adored by my family, supported in friendship, encouraged by my clients and inspired within a kinship of healers.

I enjoyed the time we spent walking on the beach, exploring the art shops, perusing the Malecon, visiting with friends for lunch and dancing in the pubs at night. Our vacation was picture perfect until March 11th when our vacation vibe was slam-dunked face first into the sand as we watched the news reporters announce that the National Basketball Association (NBA) had suspended the 2019-2020 season. Reports of quarantines, stay-at-home orders, curfews and other disease control measures flooded every television station and filled the world with fear. COVID-19 fears sent travelers into a frenzy as they rushed to prepare for the possibility of shortages and the mass spread of what was quickly being referred to as a pandemic.

When we returned home from Mexico a few days later, I felt like I had been sent to my room until I learned to behave and stayed for days refusing to come out. I struggled to wear a mask, and my hands burned when I used hand sanitizer. My refusal to inject the viral control serum was a choice that had me feeling like a transgressor in a world filled with judgment. Admitting that I had done something wrong was a lie I refused to admit.

View my special message by scanning the code below OR go to: https://qrco.de/27_2020Vision

Chapter 28

Shut Your Toilet!

The Great Timeout in 2020 and 2021 brought me to a place where I once again felt subservient and undervalued. I worked for a family-owned landscaping company as an administrator when COVID came knocking on the door like an uninvited guest that stayed for way too long. The chaotic fear and mayhem within the company became detrimental to my mental health and well-being. After consulting with my family doctor, I resigned.

My heart felt heavy when I was junked by the family-run enterprise. I was discarded like the garbage in the lunchroom without any care or concern for my emotional health, physical wellbeing or spiritual wholeness. I knew I needed to shift into a better feeling place where I could see my own worth.

I dug into the root of my feelings and found emancipation by asking myself a question. When did I feel like I had been a slave and thrown away like trash? I looked back with kindness and compassion for myself and saw the bootlicking experience of my marriage.

The expectation of the marriage agreement was that I would be a *good wife*. Terry expected me to clean toilets, change diapers, make meals, and balance cheque books while I looked well-put-together, stayed fit, energized and able to be the hostess with the mostest. That was not feasible.

I was underappreciated, devalued, treated like a second-class citizen and spoken to with utmost disrespect. This was not the life I'd intentionally mapped at the beginning of my career when I was nineteen.

When I graduated NAIT, Northern Alberta Institute of Technology, with honors in Secretarial Arts, I saw the beauty of possibility. I upgraded a year later and achieved mastery in Business Administration. I hadn't looked ahead into my life and saw that my fairytale world would be filled with foul-mouthed insults. I did not see a life that would be shattered by words spoken by the person who'd promised to love and cherish me until death do us part. I did not suspect that, "Shut your toilet!" and "Shut your pie hole!" would be responses from the man who'd asked me to dedicate my life to him.

I looked at my career life between 1988 and 2021. I understood the patterns in my behavior and identified how I had allowed myself to be treated as less than divine. Blaming others for my mistakes made for bad business. The business of healing required me to be honest, vulnerable and raw. I dug deeper into my memory bank and saw more pain.

I saw corporate mismanagement in the businesses I had been employed by. I remembered how Terry validated his financial malfeasances like he justified his cruelty. He talked around the truth explaining that it was a necessary action for his success. The problem was that only he benefitted. His advantages were many. Boats were acquired, lavish vehicles were purchased for his new wife and children. Property was bought, renovated and sold. He bought plenty with Gold Digger Brenda and sold while the market was rich.

When I called him to discuss the balance of the money owed to me, he told me to, "listen carefully" reminding me that he was in control, and I would only be paid if I behaved. My behavior didn't change his spending. He continued to spend lavishly and renovate his penthouse in Mexico.

When his marriage to Gold Digger Brenda failed, he sold off assets to pay her settlement and invested what was left in his next business adventure. Mary Jane crops were his big business plan. Marijuana was a budding business in British Columbia, and he could not compete with the big growers. His inability to successfully manage his newest acquisition led to his next failure.

I was left unpaid once again with a pocket full of empty promises. I told him that I was tired of being treated like a sucker fish. I reminded him I was a human being and was not put on this earth to do his bidding. I told him he had belittled me for too long.

His answer was, "You owe me for making you the fighter you are."

I owed him nothing. I had become a survivor because of the self-healing I prioritized. A big part of my healing was financial and emotional wellbeing.

The spring lockdown isolation forced me to stay at home more. Each time I put a mask over my mouth, I felt suffocating anxiety surface as flashbacks carried me into the memories of my abuse. I increased my meditation practice to help me use my breath to slow my racing heartbeat. I studied each disturbing sudden vivid memory and cooled it with my breath. Breathing helped me see the experience with greater clarity.

Meditation gifted me with time to reflect on my financial mindset. Anger left untreated had grown like a hidden ember in a forest when the wind blew. I combed through the memories in my mind searching for leftover coals of rage that might flair up again.

I found the dark black coal from the enigmatic Gold Digger Brenda. I only knew her through the stories I have been told. We have not met face to face. The thought of her created claw-like seething. I searched for a way to release the irritation. I pulled out my essential oils and poured lavender onto my palms.

I inhaled the floral scent and breathed into the hatred. I stayed with my breath until I was able to feel my shoulders soften, relax, and then drop away from my ears. My heart opened and revealed the depth of my scorn.

Then, I wrote my list of grievances against her. I fueled the fire for forgiveness. I added each complaint and objection that I felt as a wife and mother. I held nothing back. When I was finished, I folded the paper in half and wrote *Let Go* on one side. I turned the paper over and scribed, *Let God*.

I placed the paper in an abalone shell, covered it in a mixture of sage, sweetgrass, cedar and tobacco. I lit a match and burned the concoction. I watched the flame and allowed my heart to connect with forgiveness. Peacefully I walked away from my past and focused on the future.

I opened my laptop and chose the song that was singing in my mind. *Rolling in the Deep* by *Adele* was the perfect song to allow me to dance away from the past toward my future. As I listened, I looked at the home that Ralph and I had built together. Selling my Newcastle house and purchasing a condominium together allowed me to reduce my debt load. Our home was exactly what we needed. Eliminating the cost of a large mortgage and time spent on yard maintenance allowed for more ease when traveling.

When you come to my home, you will realize that the bathrooms are sparkly and pristine. I likely cleaned the bathroom either yesterday or today. I scrubbed the toilet, shined the mirrors, polished the tap and organized the countertop because it was part of my ritual. I also looked in the mirror and saw my beauty.

I understood the powerful woman who had transformed her rage into kindness. The lady who looked back at me had once been a different kind of cleaner. When I was married to Terry, I was angry, vengeful, terrified and unaware. I took his toilet; his toothbrush, and I married them together. I would scrub the toilet with his toothbrush and throw it in the garbage. Then, I would place a sparkly brand new one in the holder.

I was petrified most of the time, frozen in my tracks like a rabbit left too long outside in the winter. I avoided getting caught by buying the multi-pack of toothbrushes at Costco. I usually buy five at a time.

Before I dyed the toilet water blue, I wondered if he smelled the stench on the toothbrush in the garbage.

"Smells like shit," he would say.

I would break out into a cold sweat and stutter with my breath.

"I... I... I don't know what you're talking about."

I hung onto to the anger and hatred within me. I had to change. I prevented myself from causing harm by putting a blue disc in each toilet because the dye on the toothbrush would give me away.

The Great Time Out gifted me more time to spend with my essential oils. I learned how each oil helped me emotionally. I applied my knowledge and created Cozy Comfort to support my friends and family who were suffering during isolation. I chose balsam fir to help ground the body, improve mood, as well as align the sacral and heart chakras. I included lavender to calm the body and relax the mind. Chamomile was the third essential that I added to increase inner peace.

Learning about essential oils allowed me to stay on course during the difficult months ahead. I knew my life was about to change in positive, wonderful ways. I trusted my angels would guide me to beautiful opportunities.

View my special message by scanning the code below
OR go to: https://qrco.de/ShutYourToilet

Chapter 29

The Choice

I confided to my counsellor that I was struggling to remember important parts of my trauma, she assured me this was because of C-PTSD, Complex Post-Traumatic Stress Disorder. She assured me that a healthy diet, supplements, exercise, meditation, yoga, journaling and frequent fun breaks were all helping me toward wellness.

I continued to curb my cravings for sweets and comfort foods with colorful fruits and vegetables. When I slipped into unhealthy eating patterns, I accepted my choice and chose to start anew the next day. Supplements helped improve my physical wellbeing and increase my positive mindset.

Yoga was my safe space. When I stepped on the mat, I focused completely on my breath and allowed the movement to open my physical and emotional body. I welcomed the tears when they flowed and celebrated my improved physical strength.

Writing helped me regulate my emotions. I began spending more time in libraries and bookstores because I felt safe sitting on the floor. When I experienced flashbacks or intrusive thoughts, I reminded myself that I was in charge of each emotion.

I felt safe on the floor in the library because as a child my mom took me to the library where she worked. Stories fed my soul and sparked my imagination as I sat in the basement of the Stanley Milner Library. I listened for hours as the librarian read. The children's library was built like a castle with a cage that housed the most magical iguana.

I was eight years old. My imaginative mind saw a friendly dragon in the cage. The staff who fed it lettuce became the knights and princesses in my fairytale world. I loved being at the library and enjoyed filling my bookbag with fantasy novels.

I spent hours in my bedroom reading. I studied the history of queens who ruled kingdoms. I understood the power of the art of war. I learned that villains could be brought to justice by knights in shining amour who wielded swords. While other girls were playing with dolls, I was preparing to be the ruler of the world.

I became the sovereign queen of my world through writing. Words helped me heal, own my story, take back my power and inspire others. Breakthrough Coaching allowed me to guide others toward healing and telling their story too. I love helping my clients understand the power of emotions and describe their fugly feelings.

I knew that the fugly feelings guided me toward the light. These were the feelings that I avoided because I was afraid to feel deep into my betrayal and abandonment. I learned to live in the light through many opportunities to write in anthologies.

I connected with a lady in Toronto, Pantea Kalhor, who asked me if I would be willing to write a chapter to help others navigate trauma to triumph. I excitedly agreed and wrote about finding joy after loss. I wrote of the trauma in my 25-year abusive marriage. I admitted that I was angry and hated the driver of the boat that killed Emily. Writing my chapter, *I Cannot Understand Normal Thinking* helped me become a mightier ruler. The *PTSD Compass* became an international bestseller.

I wrote of strength, healing, peace, joy, and the other side of pain because I hoped the boat driver would reach out to me. I prayed for a phone call or a text message that would allow me to confront either the lady who swore she drove the boat or the man I suspected.

I soldiered on down the road to joy even though neither contacted me. The road was not paved with glitter and gold. I was not escorted by knights in shining armor. I did not ride a magical unicorn. I carried my pen and journal that became my sword and shield. I dug deeper into my psyche and continued to confront every dark thought and scary monster.

I chose to be guided by a more shamanic, holistic approach because traditional medicine offered prescriptions that numbed the pain without offering solutions. Naysayers doubted the forms of healing I used because they had yet to try alternative forms of healing. I listened to their concerns and explained my choice.

The more I changed my mind set, the less I resonated with the victim mentality I often found in the 12-step meetings I attended. My frustration grew into a war cry as I listened to more talk of the addict than of us, the wretched souls who were beaten down by their crack-infested lives. The meetings that once inspired me became an irritation. Once again, I turned to my counselor, who suggested I take a break and try to find a different support system.

I prayed for guidance and wrote in my journal. I told my angels exactly what I wanted. My mind filled with ideas, and I began to see crystal clear what my next step was. I researched different podcasts and knew beyond a shadow of a doubt that I wanted to interview leaders in life who made a difference.

Podcasting became my passion. I watched and learned from my favorite hosts and guests. I imagined what I wanted and waited for an opportunity to be a guest on someone's show.

While I waited, I baked and prayed that I could find a way to forgive both Terry and the boat driver. I rolled chocolate chip cookie dough into balls and talked out loud. I battled every angry thought in my mind by speaking it out loud. I spoke to Jesus and begged him to guide me.

Please, help me understand why my children must still suffer?

Please, tell me when will I receive justice for the pain I have endured?

Please, show me how I will manifest the money I need to finance my dream?

What day will it be when I am able to forgive?

No one spoke back to me. I accepted the silence and continued to bake. I placed two trays of cookies into the oven and set the timer. I poured myself a glass of water and walked out onto my deck.

I opened my journal and wrote a letter to Terry. I poured my anger onto the page first. Anger had been hijacking my thoughts and was taking a real toll on my mental health. I knew that that it was important to deal with my rage so that I would stop causing harm to myself.

I wrote of the ways I felt he should have been as a husband and a father. I told him why I resented him and understood how often I had given away my power and control. I told him how often I felt embarrassed by his actions and recognized that his behavior discredited his reputation and not mine. Each sentence helped me unburden my heart. I was feeling more empowered and had become a slightly better version of myself.

When the timer rang to remind me that the cookies were baked, I went into the kitchen feeling better. I transferred two trays out of the oven and a couple more in. I set another timer and returned to the deck. I opened my journal to write another letter. This letter was to his mother.

I spoke to her about my outrage at the injustice of my divorce. I poured every petty grievance onto the page. Knowing that she would never read the letter allowed me to spread my gut-wrenching pain onto the page. I told her of my loneliness and rejection as though I was confiding in an old friend. I felt more galvanized with every page I scribed.

When the timer rang, I smiled. I felt fabulous as layers of iron and steel melted away from my heart. I walked into the house feeling lighter. When I placed two more trays on the counter, I laughed because I had baked cookies like I did when Emily was in elementary school. Bake sales always brought out the competitor in me. I beamed because I knew that competition was silly. Collaboration was much more fun.

I turned the kettle on to brew myself a nice cup of tea. Tea reminded me of the time spent with Leslie. I spent many Sunday nights drinking tea and playing bingo with Tracy, Heather, Leslie and the clan of her loyal ink dabbing friends. Bingo was church and treasured as such in the family I married into. I was so excited to join in with the ladies in waiting: mother, sister, next door neighbor, and all the ladies in the debutante club who went several times a week. Being a part of their circle of friendship meant acceptance and I longed for their approval. They lined up early in the morning to purchase the early bird specials, mid-afternoon regular games, evening bonanza and Nevada tickets. If there'd been a twenty-four-hour option, I'm certain they'd have opted in.

The rules were simple, and I would be beaten with the witch's broom if I dared to fail. Only buy as many cards as you can handle, dab first, gab second, and never, ever tell anyone how much money you spent. Secrets protected the ladies who dug into their wallets and bought five, ten, twenty, or thirty more cards as they chased their losses. Massive amounts of cash were gambled in hopes of winning the big one.

I wrote my letter to Leslie and told her about the humiliation I felt when Terry married Brenda. I composed a letter that began with heaviness of heart and ended with compassion. I explained why I wasn't willing to gamble. I divulged my plan to never settle for less than I deserved.

I closed my journal and returned to the kitchen. I dumped my tea down the drain and laughed as I heard the answer.

Forgiveness does not change the past. Forgiveness enlarges the future.

I felt a lightness of being because I had unburdened my heart. I surrendered the outcome and trusted that my angels would bring me opportunities to meet kindhearted collaborators who would share my passion. I knew that what mattered most was creating a platform that would share my message.

I looked at my life and saw that I was happier than I had been when I was married. I knew that the rightness I was seeking had begun to come into my reality. I trusted that one day all the money that I was owed by my ex-husband would be repaid. I let go of the how and banked on my angels. I knew that they would help me create more abundance in my life.

I saw how I could manifest the money I needed to finance my dream. I wrote the mission statement for my podcast.

What Matters Most podcast is my platform that showcases heartfelt conversations that offer soulful solutions.

Sparkles of spirituality bring a magical magnificence to every episode.

Each special guest has learned from life's challenges.

Together we learn to live a life that matters and create positive change in our worlds.

My mission is to share these magnificent people with the world.

Each episode offers incredible insight to help you build the person you want to be.

What day will it be when I am able to forgive?

Today was the day that I was able to forgive. Unburdening my heart opened space for possibility, compassion, trust, positive expectation and more joy.

THE CHOICE

View my special message by scanning the code below
OR go to: https://qrco.de/TheChoice

Chapter 30

Falling Forward

My mother lived in the first-floor condo we purchased in March 2018. The convenience of living in the same complex as her allowed me to attend to what she needed in addition to what provincial home care allocated. Being able to protect and advocate for my mother was one of my greatest gifts and most challenging struggles.

The long-term effects of her AVM (Arteriovenous malformation) and subsequent craniotomy (a surgical procedure in which a portion of the skull, known as a bone flap, is temporarily removed to access the brain) had left her more dependent on me as she aged. I did whatever needed to be done for her and assured her that she was never a problem.

Cooking diners assured that she didn't strain her physical body and provided healthy meals. Picking up her prescriptions and groceries alleviated her struggle with having to manage with one arm and the toll of walking and maintaining balance.

My mother's right side is weak because here brain was injured on the left side. This means that she struggles to walk and sometimes slides off her easy chair when she is trying to stand. At times I became frustrated and impatient with her disability.

One of the most heartbreaking experiences was when one day she mistakenly leaned on a sign in front of the bank. The sign was a flexible disabled parking guidepost designed to fold upon impacted with a car. When mom held onto it for support, it bent, and she fell injuring her face, arm, shoulder, hip and knee.

When I went to see mom after work, I saw the bruises and scrapes on her face. I was shocked and overcome with frustration. I immediately lowered onto one knee beside her. In that moment, I knew that Grace offered me two options— red pill or blue pill. The red pill held the promise of pain, the blue pill held the promise of patience. I took them both because I knew that pain offered healing and patience helped me practice empathy.

"Oh mom, did you fall?" I asked. My eyes filled with tears.

"I made a mistake," she explained.

As I listened to her tell me the details, I practiced compassion, forgiveness, gratitude and surrender. Mom told me that she went to the bank to pay her bills. When she exited the taxi, walked up the wheelchair ramp near the door and waited in line for her turn to go in, she felt a shortness of breath. As she lowered the surgical mask on her face to allow for more air intake, balance became a problem, and she reached for the disability sign for stabilization.

"I should have been more careful," she said.

I placed my hand and mom's knee and loving replied, "You did the best you could mom."

I asked trying to understand the situation more clearly. "Did the taxi driver tell you that you had to wear a mask?"

Mom nodded. "I told him the damn thing was a nuisance," and he said that if I didn't wear it, I couldn't get in his car.

COVID safety measures were still in place which included mandatory masking, six feet distance and use of hand sanitizer before entry. Every security measure compromised my mom's ability to transport her impaired physical body into the bank. I felt myself becoming increasingly frustrated with the situation and knew that it was important for me to find a way to help her avoid any further harm.

I took the next step and assessed mom's injuries as she continued to tell me more of the details surrounding her fall. Bruising began where the left side of her face must have hit the pavement and continued down her side to her ankle. Scrapes were evidently aged because they had scabbed over and become infected.

When I asked my mom what day the fall happened, she told me it wasn't a fall. Her insistence that the sign was the cause allowed her to place blame on an inanimate object. I chose not to argue and continued to hold back the tears.

Home care arrived to help mom with her medication and to warm up the meal that I had moved from the freezer into the fridge. Ensuring that there were enough frozen meals for mom meant having her freezer full and a minimum of fourteen backup options in my icebox too. Large flake oatmeal, fresh vegetables, boiled eggs, chicken wieners, apples, oranges, grapes, cheese, crackers, yogurt and liverwurst were staples that I ensured were in her kitchen too.

Jennifer, the healthcare aid (HCA) who brought mom her meal was a kind lady with limp whose family lived in Jamaica. Her love for my mom was evident in every action she took and word she spoke.

"I'll be back in a beet to get you ready for bed. You stay in dis easy chair and wait for me to help you get dressed for bed.

You leave the dishes on the table next to you. I will clean up when I get back. I don't want you fallin' and Nancy havin' to call the ambulance man to lift you up tonight."

I smiled at Jennifer and asked her if she knew how many days ago mom had fallen.

"It's been three days Miss Nancy, and I told your mama to call you on the phone."

I felt a rush of guilt fill my chest and my eyes well up with tears. Four days ago, mom had called me in the middle of the night because she fell getting out of bed to go to the washroom. I called 911 because I needed help lifting her up from the floor. I was late to work the following morning and needed to work late for the next two days to set up in the new products in the system. I felt awful that I had prioritized work and didn't come and check on mom.

She turned to mom and with loving sternness said, "Miss Alice you can't be letting pride stop you from calling your daughter. The good lord gave you Nancy to take care of you like you been taking care of her since she was a little."

I appreciated all the subtle answers that Jennifer had given me. God had delivered us an angel in Jennifer, and I knew that the chain of events had a very important purpose.

Jennifer gently touched mom's shoulder and smiled lovingly as she looked into her eyes. She turned to me and said, "Miss Nancy, you done be doing too much for your mama. It's okay that you not be here every night."

I smiled and took a deep breath to calm myself. I knew that I could cry later when I returned to my own suite on the fourth floor. I needed to keep my focus on my mom and look at

164

the situation with one goal in mind. What did I need to do next to ensure that mom was ready for the next phase of care.

I sat with mom for a few more minutes and helped her choose a television program that would help her rest easy until Jennifer returned. I looked at the clock on the table next to mom to see how long it would be before her bedtime. When I turned to look at mom, I saw that she had fallen asleep.

I kissed her on the forehead before I quietly left the sitting room. Before I returned to my upstairs suite, I looked around the living room, dining room and master bedroom thinking about what to move into mom's one bedroom assisted living suite. Even though mom wanted to stay in her apartment condo, I needed to continue the process of finding her the perfect senior's care facility before Christmas.

View my special message by scanning the code below
OR go to: https://qrco.de/FallingForward

Chapter 31

Communication

Planning adventures with Ralph became my priority in April of 2022 after he lost hearing in his left ear. Sudden sensorineural ("inner ear") hearing loss (SSHL), commonly known as sudden deafness, is an unexplained, rapid loss of hearing either all at once or over a few days. SSHL happens because there is something wrong with the sensory organs of the inner ear.

The frustration of a diagnosis that offered no cure was devasting. We were told that one day his hearing may return and there was no guarantee he would ever regain his hearing. I was filled with frustration and angry at a medical system that offered no definitive answers.

The trauma of Ralph's hearing loss altered our lives dramatically. His external world changed because pinpointing the direction of sounds became increasingly difficult. I became his locator and helped him understand if sounds were from the left, right, front or back. He became mentally and physically exhausted from the stress.

I felt a strong desire to fix all of Ralph's hearing-related problems and control any external stimulation that would cause him increased anxiety or stress. Within less than two weeks I relapsed into codependency. I began to persistently worry about his well-being and avoided honest communication about my feelings to prevent conflict. I put his needs before my own and neglected my well-being. My attempt to manage my own anxiety by internalizing my angst led to headaches and fatigue.

Old hurts melded with suppressed emotions, and I became irritable. When Ralph raised his voice because he couldn't hear me, I felt the stir of remembering when Terry yelled at me. The anger within me was stirred and I was ready for a fight. I knew that I needed to reach out to my healing community for help.

I welcomed healing hands to help me understand, reframe, act from compassion and learn to clearly communicate differently. Healers knew how to see into my akashic records, clear my confusion, amplify my energy and cut the energetic chords. Even though I had healed from the hurt of decades of abuse, the trauma from the most recent past had activated emotional pain within me. I focused on my own healing because I knew that I needed to let go of any and all connections to Terry.

Spirit offered me a glimpse of what our future could become if we didn't learn to communicate differently. I saw our relationship explode like a planet into a million little pieces. I knew the blast would cause a dramatic transformation that would affect our entire family. The explosion would generate powerful shock waves that ripple into the lives of our children and grandbabies. The potentially devastating effects on every one of our loved ones would alter their orbits, causing impacts, or leading to secondary collisions. A shock wave would be generated that had the potential to shatter the life we had into a million pieces. How we chose to deal with this challenge was either a make or break it decision. We could either build a beautiful new life or allow this crisis to destroy our happiness.

I worried that Ralph would sink into depression. He told me about his worries, feelings of shame, doubts about his ability to heal and fear of losing me. I reassured him that we would find a way to work through every obstacle that this painful catastrophe brought to us. My optimism was not always the answer to the sadness, rage, anger and irritation he felt. I learned to allow him to openly express his feelings while working through the challenges I faced.

When he spoke the volume and intensity of his voice increased. I told him he was yelling at me and asked him to lower his voice. Silence followed and I was faced with a quiet that activated an inferno of rage within me. The absence of sound brought me to a place that felt terrible. I did the only thing I could do and faced my greatest fears with my eyes closed. Meditation became my solace.

I could not meditate in the space that held his anger. I allowed him to sulk on the couch and retreated to the safety of my office. I leaned into my own pain and saw the hidden wounds within my heart. Each memory that surfaced in my mind showed me where I needed to heal. I knew that I could use his challenge to enter the dark spaces in my heart.

Journalling helped me articulate what I could not speak. I emptied my heart onto the safety of the pages and allowed myself to fully express my pain. I was angry with God for once again bringing pain into my life. I honestly and openly shared my feelings and asked my angels to help me to conquer this challenge.

Overcoming meant adapting to the challenges that I faced while allowing him the space to be alone. We each needed to have the space for grace to help guide us. I did not know what Ralph needed. I only knew how to understand my own needs. I took the time to meet with my heavenly council and ask them to show me where I needed to heal. I asked the archangels to guide me and welcomed them to join me.

Archangel Raphael appeared before me, placed his hands on my heart, encouraged me to breath deep and filled me with a soft green light. I began to unburden my heart and felt a lightness of being within. Each breath I took allowed the light to brighten. I visualized the radiant energy penetrating my skull and course through my veins and every organ. I felt the love in my heart expand and knew that compassion, tenderness, kindness and respect were the actions needed. Love was the answer to all of my fears.

When I opened my eyes, I saw the beauty around me in the home we had created together. I was grateful for the perfectly mismatched mixture of Ralph's way of being and mine. Organization and simplicity were complimented by a comfortable, disorganized flow of constant creation. Pictures of our family were on bookshelves lined with hundreds of my books. My projects were neatly organized in colorful totes filled with binders. I saw through the eyes of love the home that love built.

I returned to the living room and saw that Ralph had fallen asleep. I covered him with a blanket and quietly walked into our bedroom. Sleep was exactly what I needed too. I cuddled under the blankets and quickly drifted off to sleep. I was transported into a world filled with all of the wonderful places we had vacationed to. The laughter of our family mixed with the sound of music playing from a rock band. I felt the water as I walked along the beach with my hand gently held by Ralph's.

I woke with a knowing that we needed to focus on what made us happy. We needed to work through our challenges, problems, obstacles and fears together. The life we had built together had an enduring love that was worth fighting for. I knew that I could be a better listener and give Ralph the space he needed to process his new normal.

Planning for future vacations always gave us purpose. Before the pandemic and the lockdowns, we had planned on vacationing longer. We vowed to extend our travel time by one week each year. The winters of 2020 and 2021 were filled with travel restrictions that prevented us from enjoying the magic of Mexico.

I knew Ralph was awake when I heard the television turn on. The volume had increased to accommodate his limited hearing. When I struggled with the loud sound, I retreated into the kitchen and cooked. Cooking brought me comfort and allowed for me to shift my energy from frustration to calm.

Trusting that this radical change in our life could be transformed with love became easier when I focused on my own healing. I scheduled self-care regularly and allowed my tribe of healers to help me release the tension in my body and restore me to the best possible version of myself. In the evenings after work, I shared my love of reflexology with Ralph and rubbed his hands and feet.

We focused on improving our communication and planned our next vacation. Watching videos about places to travel in Mexico fueled our passion for travel. Committing to more travel allowed us to focus on the future that we had committed to create together.

View my special message by scanning the code below
OR go to: https://qrco.de/31_Communication

Chapter 32

Mourning More

Monday morning coffee was different the day I woke and remembered Ralph's mom had been gone for one year. One special memory with Ortenzia jumped to the forefront of my mind to indicate that it had something important within it. Spirit had a very direct, repetitive, way of whispering to me and showing me where within the memory to focus. First, I saw Ralph's parents walking before me. Then, I was walking beside Ralph and his mom Ortenzia. We joined hands with Ralph's dad to form a circle that represented family.

The message was a reminder that we loved and lost. It was also a communication from spirit expressing the power of the circle of love. Even though mom's physical presence was no longer with us, her heavenly love could still be felt. I acknowledged the pain of not hearing her voice and feeling her touch.

Grief is not something we get over. Grief is a remembrance and missing that never ends. To deny this is to deny the truth.

I think of you on your special day. This is the day you left. The day I never imagined. The days that followed were a blur. The calls to family to tell them who could and could not come to the funeral were awful. Preparations for death masked in the restrictions that didn't allow us to honor your life.

Here I was a year later in 2022, remembering all that you gave us with your special love. The lady who loved life so very much. The special flower called Ortenzia which means hydrangea. Eighty-one beautiful years of life. My mother-in-law who didn't remember my name.

Dementia is a dreadful disease that robs the mind. The hands of this horrendous condition touch so many of our lives. When I watched my loved ones suffer with Alzheimer's and Dementia, I wondered who else will struggle to remember. Will my own memory dissolve as I walk the path of unknowing?

When I missed my beloved Emily and all of those who went before and after, I went to the garden of longing. I've been there many a time. I travel there to see her smiling face and hold her hand. We walk the paths where flowers bloom and watch the butterflies. We share some childhood memories of yesterday's gone by. Each time I miss another, I meet them in the garden with her. Sweet daughter, dear friend, you have brought me so much comfort and wiped so many tears since you went away.

Our lives changed so much without you here to share with us or feel your gentle touch. We miss your smile, your laughter, too. We miss those days gone by. We often sit and wonder about the reasons why. We guess your light was needed on the other side of life and that God needed you to help with the great plan.

Bonds of love cannot simply break. The love experienced cannot be severed by death. Each memory holds a place in the space of our hearts that distance creates. The circle of love cannot be destroyed.

Ralph's mother's dementia began when she was sixty-nine years of age, which was before I knew her. Her long-term memories held strong to the family she loved. Ralph and his ex-wife Brenda were part of those sixty-nine years.

I didn't mesh with the tapestry of her life. Each time I came to visit her, she asked Ralph about Brenda. Each time, he explained he was divorced. I was the girlfriend—the ghost and the smile. Together, we made memories as I held her hand and smiled.

During the years I spent with Mom, I picked her lilacs because she loved their scent. We walked in the beautiful gardens of the sacred pyramids in the river valley that houses a multitude of flowers. We kept a keen eye on Mom who wandered and got lost. Family gathered together as the disease progressed. Decisions were made for long-term care.

Mom's journey in long-term care was filled with loving people and beautiful memories. Anna, Ralph's sister, visited her often to ensure that she was happy and well cared for. Ralph's father visited daily.

I did what I could until I couldn't do anything. Our anything was robbed when the great reset came.

The separation from Mom behind masks and glass was a cruel experience. Mom lost her ability to speak English and fell back into the comfortable world of Italian. The staff were not fluent, and Mom fell through the crack of Covid. Ask me why I believe in self-sovereignty, freedom, choices and advocacy and I will tell you my mother-in-law's name is Ortenzia.

When death came, family loved each other. As Mom's body withered, our hope held strong. Death came and carried her to the others side where angels waited. You are forever in our hearts. You are always on our minds. We will continue to speak your name and tell your story.

MOURNING MORE

View my special message by scanning the code below
OR go to: https://qrco.de/MourningMore

SCAN ME

Chapter 33

Spring Court

In April 2023, I supported Nikita, my niece, and Tania, her mother in family court. I sat in the Kelowna court room listening to the trial hoping that they would receive a judgment that would give them emotional and financial closure.

My reason for being present was to honor the vow I made to Nikita after Emily died. I promised to always love and support her during her challenges and obstacles. Helping her see the greatness within herself was very important to me.

As I sat in the courtroom, I wondered why the opposing party, my ex-brother-in-law, David, who was Nikita's father, fought so long against Tania. I couldn't understand why he hated Tania so much that he would begrudge his daughter.

Terry's brother had never been a close relative. We seldom spent any time together during the twenty-five years I was in a relationship with his brother.

Tania and I had become like sisters. I knew that she was not a perfect person, nor did she profess to be. Her love for me was generous and she always made time for me when I visited Kelowna. She faithfully added flowers to Emily's memorial wreath that hung on the Eldorado dock. The pictures she sent to me helped me heal during the difficult years that I struggled with the pain of her absence.

I knew that Nikita was a kind caregiver who babysat my granddaughters. She'd managed to complete high school

177

and continue to university. Her ambition was truly a cut off chromosomes she shared with her mother.

I listened to the arguments from each side and prayed for a peaceful resolution. What I saw was seething rage that saturated David's ever-aging face and body. The middle-aged successful man I'd once admired for his determined tenacity had become an old man with restless resentment. He had been dragged before the court for over fifteen years, battling about finances for a child he barely admitted to having. If he were the type of father to carry pictures of his precious princesses, Nikita's portrait would be nestled next to his other two daughters. Sadly, Nikita didn't honor her father like his other daughters. She would not bend at the knee dutifully pledging her allegiance to the king.

I can only imagine how Nikita felt having her father's sister on his side once again. All I could do was sit beside my niece and behind her mother. Supporting those I love was important to me.

During the few hours Tania had to self-represent, she was able to plead her case. David's lawyer voiced his arguments. The judge's decision was to schedule two more days for continuation.

Nikita did not return to court. She decided her time was better spent on her studies and preparing for exams. I returned for both days and sat on the left side of the court room while David and his family sat on the right. As both sides pled their case, I journalled about how I felt as I listened to the dialogue. Both party's words activated a heart wound within me. The extended family who shared many of my birthday celebrations refused to look at me as they walked to and from the witness chair. Eyes were lowered when they exited the room and if their heads were raised, they averted their eyes or looked right through me. I didn't expect hugs or a parade for our family reunion. The cold shoulder felt familiar and yet I was still impacted by the disdain.

Tania and I returned to her condominium after court and cooked dinner. When Nikita came home from school, I sat and listened to her explain the classes she was taking and her plans for the future. She spoke with a wise, keen, intellect that showed her passion for learning and strong desire to continue onto university. Each day after court, I looked forward to her company. We shared an interest and understanding about the psychology of social media and history courses she was taking. I gratefully accepted her request to review her history essay and offered suggestions for improvement.

Managing school, work, daily chores and networking with friends was a challenge for Nikita. Anxiety, overwhelm, doubt and worry took away from her cheerful, creative, optimistic and faithful demeanor. I brought her a few of my essential oil roller ball creations to help her manage her emotions. Peaceful was one of her favorites because it helped her ground, anchor in peace, feel more secure and stable as she continued to face the challenges in her life.

I left Kelowna with a heart full of love knowing that the time spent with Tania and Nikita made a difference and solidified my commitment to always remain a constant in their lives. Even though the court case did not offer resolution, I was grateful that I could once again offer my support and return for the next trial date.

View my special message by scanning the code below
OR go to: https://qrco.de/SpringCourt

Chapter 34

Defeated

Spirit, the source of all life and the essence
of every soul, gifted me with the word "defeated" on the
12th day of June 2023. I heard the word while dreaming and
understood its meaning. I saw myself throw one rock at the
giant and defeat him. Bravery, courage and faith were lessons I
was to learn in the next chapter of my life.

I repeated the word until I was able to write it down in the
journal that I kept on my desk. The message within the dream
could be understood best if I chose to reflect on it before my
mind began to replay yesterday, fast forward to tomorrow and
everything in between. For me, being defeated is the feeling
between giving up and continuing to trudge through the day.
When I wanted to give up and stay in bed, I knew that I was
close to calling work and telling them I was too sick to come in.
The truth that I was sick and tired of sacrificing my happiness
made me angry.

Anger gave me the power to get out of bed, step forward
with determination, believe that my dream needed to be
prioritized and decide to get my carcass out of the coffin. I knew
that if I stayed in bed, I would become depressed and accept
the death of my dream. I rejected the belief that I had no control
over my life and chose to deal with the yuck fuck of doubt that
temporarily troubled me. If I hesitated to get out of bed, my
ability to unravel the meaning of my dream would be sabotaged.

I chose to face my lack of faith with a sword and a shield.
My sword was gratitude, and my shield was my belief in

myself. I remembered my dream to build a business that was in alignment with my love of writing. Giving thanks would help motivate me to move beyond the aggravation of my day.

Last night my phone lit up with messages from work listing what I was expected to accomplish. The never-ending demands that included reminding my boss to transfer funds from one bank account to another, email last week's e-transfer list to the team, check the exchange rate for Canadian and United States dollar, reconcile the credit card statements and input all new items into the data base. My to do list for one day was enough for an entire week or two full-time employees.

I needed to reframe my thoughts and focus on how I was going to retire from the mayhem of the job that was paying my bills. The reward of focusing on my divine plan would help me heal cell- and soul-deep.

I gritted my teeth, sat up, grabbed my phone, and dragged my body to the bathroom. Pee, wipe, turn coffee maker on, then shower are parts of my routine to keep moving forward toward meditation and journalling. I knew that the answer to the word defeated would find me when I sat in my office.

I dressed in jeans, tank top, long sleeve shirt and zip-up hoodie. I needed to dress in layers to ensure that I followed the dress code at work. I was required to keep my arms and tattoos covered as well as ensure that I had jeans on for safety. The extra layers were to keep me warm because my coworker's response to hot flashes was a fan running in the office all day.

I poured myself a cup of coffee and walked into my office to spend time unravelling the mysterious word from my dream. The process began with deep breathing to help me connect with my angels, the ascended masters, archangels and my loved ones who had crossed to the other side of the veil. The deeper I breathed the clearer their presence became. I loved how I could name each of the spirits who graced me with their presence.

As always, my sweet Emily came to sit beside me. The ascendants that came to guide me that day were Kwan Yin, Jesus, his mother Mary and Enoch. I was honored and grateful for their love. I began to see my morning in the light of truth.

I saw yesterday's trust become today's promise as the sunrise began to glow. The sun welcomed me to this day and once again I smiled. I wondered how I became so lucky and laughed. I'm not lucky, I am blessed.

First, I learn and then I earn has been my mantra for over a decade. When I didn't know how, I pressed my hands together in prayer and began to breathe. I closed my eyes and allowed my breath to guide me.

My angels gathered around me until I was able to let go of the worry. I felt hands on my back, shoulders, chest and brow. The space between brows softened as my third eye opened to see beyond the veil.

No longer did I fear the images that filled my mind. When the ascendant masters appeared, I asked them to tell me who they were. As my mind filled with messages, I thanked Spirit for helping me learn their names. He who helps God and is full of Grace blanketed me with his pale, yellow, almost egg-white color. It was his love that helped me with transition, grief and loss. Archangel Azrael was my comforter.

He appeared before me wearing a cloak after Emily died. I feared "the angel of death" until I asked him to reveal himself. He removed his hood, and I saw a purple, golden and red aura.

I knew that he was with me to help me through the transition from administration to leadership.

The message that filled my mind's eye was, "It's always okay. Your time in this space and time is temporary. You will move away from this mortal struggle. Allow the pain to come and remember to breathe. This too shall pass."

If I believed that anything was possible, I would be able to wait until my angels guided me to the meaning of defeated. My next call to action was to ask Archangel Michael to help me with the sword of truth. I knew that he could help me remove the barriers of fear, the cords of the past and those chains that bound me to anger.

His beautiful cobalt-blue aura surrounded me and gave me the insight I was looking for. He showed me a young shepherd boy who faced a giant. The young boy's name was David, and his opponent was Goliath. I saw the battle that was won miraculously by an underdog who, against all odds, should not have won at all.

The improbable victory was possible because Goliath did not anticipate David's extraordinary abilities. The giant did not have the intuitive insight and faith that the young shepherd boy carried inside of him. Goliath's greatest weakness was that he did not see the power of David's courage and faith. Instead, he saw before him a child with a sling and a rock. The giant was defeated by his own arrogance.

I understood the message and thanked my angels for their assistance. I promised myself that I would take a risk doing something that I was passionate about rather than feel lost not doing what I love. I vowed to defeat the giant fear that was inside of me. I prayed to my angels to help me escape from the corporation that was governing over me.

I asked the Dream Weaver to grant me an opportunity to exit my career in administration with grace. The tug of war between me and the managers was exhausting. I was no longer able to relax, sleep well, exercise and restore my body or mind after work. I wanted to leave the drama behind and create a way of life that was filled with love instead of sadness.

I asked Jesus to help me orchestrate an orderly and uneventful departure, timed so as not to detract from my wellness or the company I was a part of. I imagined being whisked away with Ralph in a starship to a beach where work and play meld into meaningful existence. I like the sound of that; I like it a lot! I wasn't looking to retire from working, creating, collaboration and purpose. I simply wanted to focus more on meaningful contributions with people who shared my mission.

I found a way to spread more joy after Emily passed because I learned that true happiness and joy were ways of being. My friends, family, clients and even strangers told me that I had a calming effect on them. I was often told there was something special about me that couldn't be explained. People often said the energy shifted when I walked into their home.

I knew that I could help parents understand that recovery from the loss of a child was possible. I proved that creating a fabulous life after suffering from abuse and battery was doable. What I needed to do was align with my purpose.

The job simply did not match my mission. I needed to find some way to quantum-leap into a future that allowed me to focus on what mattered most. Call me silly, but I believed that I could change the crappy, self-sabotaging programs playing repeat in my life.

Instead of rushing off to a job that did not satisfy me, I pulled out a poster board, magazines, markers and glue.

Creating a vision board was exactly what I needed to complete to clarify what my island of peace looked like. I focused on the feelings of happiness, self-confidence, wellness and determination. Playing with markers reminded me of time spent with my granddaughters. I began to giggle and sprinkle sparkles all over the vision board.

A flash of insight came into my mind, and I suddenly knew exactly what I needed to do. Being more childlike was the solution to my dilemma. I knew the corporate culture of the company I worked for did not allow the joy that I needed in my life. Too often I was chastised for my lack of professionalism, which included laughing too loud, being silly, talking to my coworkers, using colored pens and excessive highlighting.

Even though I respected my manager, who was also one of the owners, I was not willing to sacrifice my well-being and happiness for her success. I knew there was a peaceful solution to every problem in my life and that this challenge needed prayer.

I walked to my yoga mat, got on my knees, prayed and surrendered all my worries to the creator. I asked my angels to help me release my guilt. I prayed for a way to manifest a change in my life. I focused on my breath until I was able to be in the present moment.

Then, the phone rang. My mother had been found unresponsive in her bathroom. Her blood pressure was low, and she was being taken by ambulance to the hospital. They told me what hospital she had been sent to and I knew in one moment exactly what I needed to do.

I texted Ralph, Jarett, Chance and Joshua as I calmly walked to my car. As I drove out of the underground parking, my phone rang. Jarett asked me to tell him what happened to Oma. As I drove west toward the Misericordia Community Hospital, my phone continued to beep with messages from work. The continual bombardment of beeps was aggravating and distracting my ability to concentrate on driving.

I pulled over and sent a message to the team that was simple and direct, "I am on my way to the hospital. My mother was found non-responsive." Then, I turned my phone off.

When I returned to driving, I began to pray. Lord Jesus please do not allow my mother to die in the same hospital I was born. Help me find a way to help her, guide me to staff who are willing to listen, be compassionate and determined to find out why her health is continuing to decline.

I felt calm, determined, focused and willing to be calm in the situation that scared me. Even though I was uncertain, I knew that I would be guided by my angels. When I entered the parking lot at the hospital, I found a space next to the emergency exit beside a tree next to a grassy area. I calmly parked, opened my purse and pulled out my cigarettes. Today was not the day to feel one whisper of guilt for enjoying a smoke.

I wanted to manifest an opportunity to leave my job without feeling guilty that my coworkers would struggle without me. I needed to eliminate the emotional and physical strains on my body and mind. Without knowing the outcome, I surrendered to my angels. I promised that I would trust their guidance and reach out to family and friends for support.

I turned my phone on and saw that work had responded with varying degrees of kindness and concern. I answered with, "thank you" and turned my phone onto silent. I focused on what matters most, which was my mother and her health.

DEFEATED

View my special message by scanning the code below
OR go to: https://qrco.de/Defeated

Chapter 35

Flash of Insight

When I walked into the emergency room entrance, I was guided to the receptionist who asked me a series of questions to ensure I had met all the requirements for entry. I confirmed that I had no symptoms related to COVID or any other infectious diseases. Then, as required by provincial regulations I sanitized my hands, picked up a mask with a set of tweezers and placed it over my nose and mouth.

As instructed, I walked down the hall, turned left twice, then right and reported to the nurse's station. The charge nurse directed me to my mother's stretcher that was in the hallway. I began to pray as I walked toward my mom who was calling out for a nurse to help her.

When my mom saw me, she immediately begged me to help get a nurse because she desperately needed to go the bathroom. I touched her on the arm, smiled with my eyes and assured her I would get help.

There were two nurses at the station who were working with the paramedic team who had just brought in another elderly patient. I waited patiently until they were done before I asked for help. Nurse number one informed me that they were busy. With compassionate resolve I assured her that I understood she was busy and would be willing to wait. I turned to the other nurse and stated that my mother was attempting to get off the stretcher by herself.

As I walked towards mom, she cried out, "Please help me. I'm going to pee my pants."

I touched mom's arm and told her that I had spoken to the nurses and that they were going to help her in a few minutes. I asked her to explain to me what had brought her to the hospital.

She told me that she had fallen. The bruises on her face and arms showed the severity of her tumble. We continued to talk while mom moaned, squirmed and tossed on the gurney. Ten minutes passed before I walked back to the nurses' station to ask if they were able to help mom.

I had learned to wait longer than I liked because my mom's paralysis made her a two-person lift. This often meant that she had to hold her pee. Urinary tract infections had become a part of the new normal that she was forced to endure.

When the ladies came to help, they were kind and apologetic. I appreciated that they called her Alice and thanked her for being patient. Finding something to be grateful for during difficult ordeals helped me work with the staff instead of freaking out.

We remained in the hallway waiting to move to emergency for over twelve hours. I was able to remain patient and stay cheerful because I had a great group of friends who were checking in on me. Every hour I would either get a cup of coffee, go to the bathroom, walk outside, send a text message or return a phone call.

One of my coworkers helped me navigate the bombardment of concerns about work. I had no idea how many days I would be with mom, and I was concerned that they would not be able to navigate the system that I had created for new items. Procurement was a huge part of my administrative role and the changes I had made to the flow were not always accepted with cooperative collaboration.

I called Jackie, who ran the sales desk, to let her know how mom and I were doing. She was able to help me see what I needed to do to not worry about work. Her words of wisdom, "Let them fuckin figure it out. You focus on your mom." were exactly what I needed to hear.

One of the greatest gifts that I have received in my life is meeting magical people. Jackie's magic was that she was both funny and wise. The more I got to know her the better I understood the champion who had endured intense trauma. I learned to be a better listener when I was with her because when she spoke her eyes showed much of her pain. I wondered what my eyes looked like and began to look more deeply into the mirror when I did my makeup before work.

I liked seeing the different reflections of my emotions each morning. When I saw the distinctive difference between unhappy work Nancy and joyful weekend Nance, I made a vow. This would be the last job I ever had where unhappiness was part of my day. I boldly wrote in my journal, "I will only work with and for people who bring me joy. I will trust the universe and all my angels to help deliver me from the hell I am living in."

When I told Jackie, she giggled and told me, "You better get a broomstick and fly your witchy ass out of this place fast before they suck all the joy out of you!" Her hilarious sense of humor was one of the only reasons I enjoyed going to work in the corporate castle. We were quite the team when we were allowed to work together, which wasn't very often because we laughed too much. I loved that we were two old horses who still have enough get-up-and-go to giddy-up and make a better workday. Happiness was our end game, and we made the most of each day whether at work or doing what we loved.

Last December after the Christmas campaign at work, I wrote in my journal about choices and change. I was becoming increasingly disheartened by the milieu at work. My coworkers were complaining to me about how unhappy they were and that they were seeking other employment. I was tired of hearing my manager tell me how things were done "back in the day" because I was focused on creating a healthier future instead of reinventing the past.

If I wanted to change my direction toward a happier more meaningful life, I needed to take an honest inventory of what I had created. Then, I needed to look at what I wanted to change.

I admitted that because I was complying with my bosses demands I was communicating agreement. I owned up to my passive aggressive behavior which included complaining to coworkers and snarky sidebar conversations during meetings. I committed to foster openness and transparent conversation with the management team in the new year. I also created a backup plan. If my manager wouldn't work with me to create a happier workplace, I would resign.

I remembered the joy of Christmas when I created the Heartfelt Handbag campaign and collected gifts for women who were spending the holiday season in shelters. Helping families who were struggling financially was important to me. Giving back at Christmas was important to me because I understood the feeling of not being able to afford to buy presents.

Working in the corporate castle did not align with joy at Christmas because we were expected to work extra hours to keep up with the retail rush. The toy campaign at work provided toys to remote areas in western Canada. When I learned about the program, I was excited to be a part of supporting families in need. What I didn't know was that I would be unable to continue my volunteer work because I was drained from the exhausting computer work and constant strain on my body.

The change I needed to make was how I generated financial wellness. I committed to creating a life that allowed me to celebrate the true meaning of Christmas. I needed to find a way to leave the retail rat race and focus on collaborating with people and organizations that were truly heart centered.

I opened my journal and wrote my plan. This time next year, I will be collaborating with organizations whose mission is in alignment with helping women in need, children who have been afflicted by violence and celebrating the joy of giving.

I focused on what my optimal future would feel like and allowed my angels to set into motion the events that would lead me. I forgave myself for choosing to sacrifice my emotional and physical wellbeing. I acknowledged that focusing on what I didn't have was taking a toll on my mental health. Thoughts of scarcity were fueling my decisions in the wrong direction.

A flash of insight filled my heart and mind. More time spent with my mom was more valuable than hours spent in the company of those who did not care for my wellbeing. Even though my manager acted as though she cared about me, the reality was she cared more about her own financial gain.

I focused on the only true reality which was the present moment. Each action I took from that day forward was with my angels. When I felt pessimistic, doubtful, fearful or overwhelmed, I made an agreement to connect with my heart instead of the draining thoughts that separated me from joy.

FLASH OF INSIGHT

View my special message by scanning the code below
OR go to: https://qrco.de/FlashOfInsight

Chapter 36

Abundance

I walked back into the hospital through the emergency room entrance, once again I was expected to follow the protocol. Even though I thought the entire process was unnecessary, I followed the steps necessary to gain access. I answered the same questions once again and this time I created a better experience. I joked with the receptionist and asked if there would be a cavity search to check for weapons. She laughed and said, "Maybe next time."

When I returned to the hallway, mom was no longer there. I smothered the fire of fear that quickly flared because I imagined the worst by walking back to the emergency department. The kind receptionist that I had joked with saw the terror in my eyes and waved me over.

She assured me, "Your mom is okay. She has been moved into a room."

The triage desk clerk directed me to the unit where mom had been moved to. When I walked into her room, she breathed out heavily and smiled.

Then she frowned and said, "I don't know why I'm here."

I smiled and sat down in the chair beside my mom's bed. Explaining the series of events that brought her to the hospital helped me ease her concern. I held her hand and told her that she had a fall, was brought to the hospital in an ambulance, had soiled her panties and was waiting to see the doctor.

"Yes, the ambulance brought me here." she replied.

"Do you know what hospital we are at mom?" I asked.

She looked around the room to see if there was some sign or indicator. "It's an old one that's for sure." was her reply.

I explained that it was the Misericordia and that we were in the emergency department. She became less agitated and then suddenly everything changed. Mom began to fuss with the blankets and complain that it was so very hot in the room.

"Can you please fix my foot?" she asked.

"Which foot mom?" I questioned as I turned to look at her feet. She was wearing the royal blue slippers with Velcro straps that allowed for easy adjustment. I turned and asked her if she wanted me to loosen them.

Mom's body stiffened and her eyes rolled back. I immediately knew she was having a seizure. I came close to her face and began to stroke it and spoke the words she needed to hear. "Mom, you're having a seizure. I'm going to call for help."

I went into triage action and called out for a nurse, identified mom's room number, name and that emergency care was needed. A team of nurses, doctors, aids and support staff came quickly.

We worked together as a team. I stayed by mom's side and allowed them to record the details of the incident. The seizure was intense and lasted a few minutes. I knew something was terribly wrong because she had not experienced a severe seizure in more than ten years.

As soon as mom regained her ability to speak, she thanked me. I held back my tears and focused on assuring her that a wonderful team of earth angels were here to help her. She smiled and nodded to communicate that she understood. I told her I was going to find the doctor and ask what I could do to help.

I walked out of her room and found the charge nurse's desk. She flagged down the doctor so we could begin discussing mom's situation. The doctor came to me immediately and introduced herself. I explained who I was and then detailed the series of events that led us to the hospital. She listened, clarified, took notes and explained the steps that would be taken to figure out the drastic change in Alice's condition.

First, we returned to mom's room so that the doctor could introduce herself. I was impressed with her incredible compassion and gentle directness. She explained to mom that she was ordering a series of tests to determine what was causing the change in her wellness.

Next, the team readied mom for a CT scan so that we would have a detailed image of structures inside her body. Mom was wonderfully compliant with all the requests and asked for only one thing.

"Can my daughter come with me?"

The doctor smiled and assured her that Nancy would be with her every step of the way. While I waited for the next step, I moved my hands slowly from the top of her head to the bottoms of her feet. Reiki allowed me to assess her energies and allow loving light to enter her physical body.

After reviewing my mom's medication, the doctor prescribed the necessary medications to hopefully prevent another episode. I sat beside mom's bedside holding her hand and praying that the angels would help the medical team find the cause of the radical change in mom's health.

I stayed with mom until the porter came to move her to the imagery department. I was able to stay by her side until they began the CT scan. When I was asked to wait outside, I sent text message updates to family and friends.

Then, I pulled my Abundance essential oil roller ball from my purse. Traveling with essential oil blends was an important part of my selfcare plan. Wearing a mask activated my anxiety and essential oils always helped me calm, ground, breathe and focus on whatever needed to be done.

My recovery plan worked when I worked the plan—such a well-known cliché. The strategies I used were far from overused, predictable or lacking in originality. Each day offered different obstacles, so my plan needed to be adaptable.

The plan that I created was a head to toe and heart to soul system that included an essential oil project to help me ground from the crazy of my mind. When I found myself over thinking with 10, 20, 40, or 60 thoughts in a minute, I knew exactly what essential oil or flower essence to use to stop the hamster wheel in my mind.

Each day my thoughts were different, and I chose the perfect blend of essential oils and flower essences. Sharing my enthusiasm, vast knowledge, practice and formal education became my passion. I used and studied over a hundred plant extracts, which are also called essentials, and flower essences. My hobby became my side hustle and joy.

I created the *Essential Oil Spreadsheet Encyclopedia* to help my friends, family, clients and anyone who wanted to learn about essential oils. The system helped me share my joy and easily access my knowledge about the emotional and physical benefits of each plant extract.

Next, I created the *Choose Joy Flower Essence Encyclopedia* to share the power of the Bach remedy system. I loved the remedies and wanted to share the many ways they help balance emotions and treat negative mental states. I knew that my system could help share my wealth of knowledge.

I trusted that God would help me share their magnificence with the world. I knew it was going to be a popular project because I couldn't possibly be the only one who struggled during traumatic experiences.

When I managed my mom's care when she needed to be hospitalized, I would often feel like 4,000 thoughts raced through my mind. Using essential oils helped me take a deep breath, calm my anxiety, manage my emotions and put back on the mask that caused me anxiety. Staying calm helped me remember the importance of working with her health care team and staying in a state of compassion.

Choose Joy Essentials began when I created my first blend called Abundance. I carefully and intentionally combined just the right amount of patchouli, cedarwood, vetiver and ginger to help regain mental grace and inner peace. Years of study gave me the ability to understand exactly what extracts to combine to assist with overthinking, excessive worry and anxiety. I chose patchouli to help release negative thoughts, cedarwood to calm and soothe away nervous tension, vetiver for a clear and revitalized mindset, and ginger to reduce mental fatigue.

I was surprised when a few minutes later a nurse came rushing out into the hall looking for me. "Nancy, your mom needs you." alerted me to the emergent change in mom's condition.

Mom was having a second much more intense seizure. I moved into action by her bedside and held her hand while offering reassurance. "Mom, it's going to be okay. You are having another seizure. Keep breathing, I'm right here with you."

As her fragile weak body flailed and her eyes rolled backwards and then side to side, I remained calm. Forty-four years of experience being my mom's support system had given me incredible confidence. Having family and friends as medical experts helped me understand the complexities of her condition.

When her body was still, the emergency room doctor asked if we talk in the other room. Our conversation was collaborative flow of respectful kindness. We respected each other's knowledge and created a plan to ensure that mom's medication was adjusted to bring her back to wellness.

View my special message by scanning the code below
OR go to: https://qrco.de/36_Abundance

Chapter 37

Seeds of Success

On the first day of July, Canada Day, in the year 2023, I began writing my truth again, one letter at a time with the clickity-clack of my writer's tablet. I opened ten journals filled with handwritten words to find the right declaration to begin. The critical Judge sat in the corner of my mind, questioning my morals and virtues once again. Well, Mama didn't raise a quitter, so I was going to do this no matter what. I picked up one leather journal and held it against my chest. I closed my eyes and prayed for strength.

Ahead me was a beautiful forest with one path. I knew that writing was my path to healing. I had to write the book that I had been thinking and talking about for ten years.

Behind me stood every faithful friend and cheerleader who'd raised their glass in all the right ways. These were the patriots who believed in my greatness, my audience of acceptance and love. These were the fabulous, festive celebrants who helped me open the page and begin writing one red word at a time.

Red pens have long been used by teachers to circle mistakes and underline errors. I used red ink to manifest my dream by writing in the present as though my success already exists. There was magic in writing my requests to the angels and allowing them to create for me. I giggled when they guided me toward what was possible.

I asked my angels to guide my hands and heart toward more of what made me happy. I closed my eyes and allowed them to show me what my future looked like from their vantage point. They showed me that I could surround myself with people who loved and supported me. They reminded me that I could walk away from the job that drained me and allow the door to shut.

What was possible was more time for what I wanted and less time for what irritated me. I put my journal down and smiled. I turned and walked to the laundry room that was also our storage space. I moved what needed to go outside onto my deck. I reorganized everything that remained into three sections. First, I boxed up what no longer made me happy which included a plastic apple slicer that constantly jammed up when I used it. Next, I moved my crock pots, mix-master, roasters and canning pots onto one shelf. I felt fabulous knowing that I could get rid of what no longer served me and keep what brought me joy.

I walked out of the laundry room and knew that I needed to reorganize my life. The root of my irritability was because I had been giving too much energy to a job that brought me no joy. I no longer felt valued by my employer. I was tired of building their dream while mine waited until I had enough time and money.

I looked at the beauty of my home. My eyes turned to the mahogany masterpiece Ralph bought me for my birthday that holds my keepsakes. On top of the closed drawer sat our wedding vows, Emily's ashes, family photos, a Bermuda shell box, some sage, an orchid in bloom, incense, and a card from my friend. Inside the drawer was incense, hookah coals, matches, and seeds for a Wellness Garden.

Seeds reminded me that anything was possible. When I struggled, my Oma used to tell me to have a little faith. She showed me how a handful of seeds could grow a garden that would feed our family.

Mother Nature watered her plants and Oma caught rain in barrels for the days when the rain didn't come. Father Sun brought the light to feed the plants. The Holy Spirit made the magic that brought the fairies in the night while Mother and Father slept.

I looked at the seeds that waited for me to plant them. Time wasn't waiting for me. Time kept on clicking on the clock toward tomorrow. I took the time that I had and began to play in the dirt and dance in the compost. The kitchen sink was clean, ready and willing to be my playpen. Gardening was where I felt close to God and my Oma, Helena Domke. Each moment I'd spent with my her had been a day in heaven for me. Her love was a constant in my life until she passed away during her hundred and first year.

In the first pot, I planted marigolds whose fragrant scent I could smell as I was transported back in time to the front yard of Oma and Opa's home in Barrhead, Alberta. Pot number two held the nasturtium whose sweet flavor I could taste. Long before I became a budding botanist, I ate the edible flowers in Oma's glorious garden. The third pot held my sacred chamomile. I loved picking the wildflower that grew in front of my Oma and Opa's home and making them tea.

After I planted the seeds, I wrote in my journal with my red pen. Each sentence helped me focus on what I wanted. More joy was my mission, and I succeeded in the most wonderful ways. I created more magic in my life too.

I designed a more colorful life. I made healthy meals with a deliberate intention to have more color. I embraced my own style with every outfit I wore and began to feel like a superhero. Every day became a fun day as I fearlessly embraced my *fugly* emotions. Fucking ugly emotions that dig deep into the dirt of my pain gave me ammunition to fire all my guns at once and explode into space. I let the fireworks explode and the waterworks fall when feelings surfaced. Burying my emotions was as dangerous as burying bodies in my garden. Eventually, I would have to dig them up and deal with them.

View my special message by scanning the code below OR go to: https://qrco.de/SeedsOfSuccess

Chapter 38

Family First

I chose to rest my right arm in August of 2023. Years of no pain, no gain mindset had not served me. My doctor declared that the tendonitis was due to repetitive strain. He warned me that the journey to restore my body to wellness would take time. How long he could not be certain.

My logical mind knew that each day I remained caused more harm to my physical body. My thumb, pointer finger and middle finger were numb. My elbow and shoulder either throbbed or filled with stabbing pain with each movement. Each key stroke and mouse move was aggravating. The pain affected my relationship with my mom because I was unable to push her wheelchair. Patience was less, irritability grew more. I felt uncertain, slightly afraid and boldly determined in the softest way. Life truly had changed since the days that I wept on the floor in my former home, Greystone.

His fortune has faded. The money that was once available to be paid to me no longer exists. His grandiose plans to buy property and develop it into a subdivision failed. The maintenance enforcement court order has failed to yield any money to me. According to the Maintenance Enforcement Program officers he has no property or assets registered to his name.

I was positive that I would no longer prioritize anyone or anything ahead of my need to heal. My body had paid the price for my self-sabotaging behavior, and I had to make a life changing decision. Either I stay in my subservient administrative career, or I commit to finishing my memoir.

My choice was solidified with a tattoo. Mom and family first were proudly written on my left shoulder. The ochre, yellow badge of pride was my newest favorite ink that adorned my arm. New beginnings in my life often started with tattoos.

Tattoos shower my body and cover scattered scars. Like my sons, I have many tattoos that decorate my arms. Each symbol celebrates a part of my journey. In one instance, I created a tapestry to show my path for completing my yoga teacher training, with seven roses symbolizing the chakras and love.

Red represents the blood bond with Jarett. Orange is for creativity which reminds me of Joshua. Yellow is for my sunshine, Chance. Green is for my darling Emily because it was her favorite color. Blue is for my father whose love is true, loyal, genuine and unconditional. Purple is for all the women in my life who cared for me after Emily died.

I have one special tattoo nestled next to the roses. A single Stargazer lily which is my favorite flower. I love the smell of the lily. Stargazers are both beautiful and fragrant—and they remind me of Emily. She taught me to pull the pollen from the filament to keep the blooms in blossom longer. The lily ties my arm to my feet, which are adorned with a garden of other flowers. The pain of that tattoo helped me remember to pull the weeds of discontent from my mind.

Jarett's arms are a massive masterpiece of ink that represents his journey. Beneath the squid whose tentacles wrap around his arm, is the scar that he carries from the boating accident. We cover what we need to heal. He has healed deeply and continues daily.

Chance's knuckles are marked with the month, day, and year of his sister's death. His arm carries the sun. Angels, darkness, and much more dance into the depth of his skin. His life changed from party boy to husband when he met Jessy because he vowed to be her forever.

When I made my decision to focus on my wellness, my sons reminded me of the lessons I had taught them. Prioritizing my self-care would allow me to spend time with family and focus on the future that served both my recovery and helping others heal form the grief and trauma in their lives. Subserviency was emancipation and I was a slave to no one. Creating a legacy of love and joy was my birthright. I was the maker of my own destiny and at the end of the day I was accountable to myself for the choices I made.

The creations I made in this world will last long after my death. My legacy was joy, and I knew I must stay the course. I knew my family would always support me during my challenges. Choosing family first meant choosing my own happiness.

View my special message by scanning the code below
OR go to: https://qrco.de/38_FamilyFirst

Chapter 39

Autumn Farewell

I returned to Kelowna in November to visit Chance and support Tania. The autumn leaves were still on the trees and Okanogan Lake was calm. I wanted to be more like the lake that worried about nothing and trusted everything. Mother Nature managed the masterpiece of water and rock. She cared for the fish and plants—her family—with effortless ease.

I wanted to learn to be calmer and more peaceful. I began listening more. Two weeks of life with my sugary, sassy granddaughters brought great revelations. I knew that I was built to love more than I was to hate.

The opportunity to heal happened when I was activated by the memories of the past. Anger had great power, and a five-minute flash of rage used up a great amount of energy. If I had toddler temper tantrum, I would end up making more of a mess in my life. When I sat in quiet reflection and breathed through the battle in my mind, I was able to see solutions.

The court case I came to witness was not my battle. I was there to offer support to my sister-in-law and niece. I was not there to cause harm or rehash the past. I could not hold onto hatred for the life I lived or the people who brought me pain if I wanted to be a vessel of peace.

I repeated the *Prayer of St. Francis* as a reminder:

Lord, make me an instrument of your peace.
Where there is hatred, let me bring love.

Where there is offence, let me bring pardon.
Where there is discord, let me bring union.
Where there is error, let me bring truth.
Where there is doubt, let me bring faith.
Where there is despair, let me bring hope.
Where there is darkness, let me bring your light.
Where there is sadness, let me bring joy.
O Lord, grant that I may not so much seek
to be consoled as to console,
to be understood as to understand,
to be loved as to love,
for it is in giving that one receives,
it is in self-forgetting that one finds,
it is in forgiving that one is forgiven,
it is in dying that one awakens to eternal life.

Seeing my ex-family in court challenged me to see through the lens of forgiveness. Their desire to rid themselves of the connective tissue that holds the heart of my niece is both fierce and foul. They don't value what they do not see the value of. Her father had not seen her for over five years. He pays the court appointed payments and offers her nothing more.

Nikita remained a part of my life because I made a conscious effort to see her. When she asked me to read and edit her scholarship essay, I agreed and encouraged her to keep applying for bursaries. Receiving a bursary allowed her to enroll in college. Even though her father withdrew his love from her life, she continues to stay committed to her dream to complete a master's degree. My hope was that he would see the value of her education and choose to support her financially.

Within my skin, deep beneath the molecules and microbes, lay my inner being. I was sunshine mixed with a little hurricane. When I was passionate about a project, I shined and if I choose to advocate for someone or something I encourage them with love. I used the hurricane energy to help the people I love. I remained in the center of storm where it is calm. I preferred to be peaceful and allow the chaos to brew around me.

Tania supported me during the bitter cold pain of my daughter's death and was my peace when I walked into the funeral home. She stayed with me during my depression and supported me during my divorce. I leaned on her until I was able to walk alone.

I walked toward my understanding of life and death. I knew that death was not the end of life. I believed that there was no death, instead, there is a change in frequency. When I chose peace, love, pardon, union, truth and faith, I was able to be in the court room next to my ex-family without anger.

Doubt did not dance in my mind when I looked at the work ahead of me. I knew my determination would pay off. Success was my only option. I let go of the need to know the exact outcome because I trusted that justice would prevail.

Each night after court, I prayed to my angels and asked them to guide me toward peaceful resolution. I surrendered and released all the fears I no longer needed to Archangel Michael who helped me cut the chords that bound me to people, places and situations. As I slept, I dreamt of a beautiful path before me where I walked protected by his light.

Each morning, I woke up early before the sunrise and enjoyed my coffee on the deck with a blanket wrapped around me. The cool morning air in November was a gentle reminder of the winter days that were coming. I wrote in my journal about the court case and my time spent with Chance, Jessy and the girls. I detailed my observations, feelings, reflections and gratitude. I asked GUS—God, Universes, Spirit—to help me cancel any and all contracts, agreements, bindings, documents, alliances, allegiances, written, verbal and non-verbal commitments with any and all persons, places and beings who are not an energetic match with me and my life purpose. Then I finished my coffee and had a shower before Chance, Jessy and the girls woke up.

My phone flashed with a comment on a post that I had made on Facebook the day before. I had written about the excellence of my son's huge residential roofing project and the joy of spending time with my granddaughters. "Must be nice to always be on vacation," was the suggestive statement that insinuated that I continually travelled the world in vacay mode.

Terry, my ex-husband, had once again thrown a muddy insult at me. This time it landed at my feet and missed the mark. I stayed in peace and gratitude while I laughed out loud. My angels had answered my request in less than an hour and that gifted me with a memory.

Before I could write a word in response, Chance walked out on to the deck and greeted me with a "Morning Momma," and a kiss on my forehead.

I happily laid down my phone and enjoyed watching my son go back into the house and get ready for work. Jessy his wife was yet to come home from her nursing night shift at the Kelowna General Hospital. I was tasked with getting the girls ready for school and Grandma Dawn was driving them.

Spending time with my granddaughters was a sweet treat for me because I only saw them a few days each year. I willingly helped out as much I could and did my best to capture as many memories as possible. Last night we snuggled watching movies, shared popcorn, colored, read bedtime stories and played hide 'n go seek.

Before Chance left, he gave me the rundown of what the girls needed for school and when they needed to be ready for pick up. He kissed me on the forehead a second time, "Thanks for helping Mama. I really appreciate it. I wish you were here all the time."

I smiled and winked, "Me too buddy." I assured him that I would have the girls ready on time and that I would also help Jessy with dinner.

When I heard the door close behind him, I opened my phone to deal with my Facebook post.

Engaging with a monster was not part of the peaceful paradise visit I had planned. Instead of arguing with his insult, I deleted his comment and blocked his profile. Then, I opened my journal and unpacked the memory that had been activated by his comment.

Years before the marijuana market crashed and the crack clouds blocked the beauty of the day, my monster offered to pay for Sunny's nanny. His generous offer was made to her maternal grandmother, Dawn, who lived two doors down the lane. Nails dig deep into my mind, Freddy-Kruger-style when I hear how Fat Daddy is willing to share his fat stack of money with another woman.

Please remember that he owes me over $800,000, and that's without adding in ten years' worth of accumulated interest. Trust that my accounting is accurate. Believe that I have exhausted all means to collect each silver dollar.

Karma had danced in my life and offered me an opportunity to cancel all written and verbal commitments or agreements with any and all persons, places and beings who are not an energetic match with me and my life purpose. Terry was definitely not welcome or wanted in my life in any way, shape or form. I successfully fought the urge to pick up the phone and dial. I hadn't spoken to him for months and had no desire to engage with his madness. What needed to be said was no longer able to be heard. His mind had been devoured by the world of hurt he had willed upon himself.

Words written on paper penetrate the perpetrator with more power. The last legal paper filed made a small dent in the empty financial equation of the money long spent. The court order will be enforced through the court of maintenance enforcement the day hell freezes over. The white winter of many snowy years chipped away at the millions he once had. I'll never know the truth of his addicted life after we divorced. I only know the truth of the trauma I experienced for two terrifying decades.

I chose to deal with my own addictions instead of his. I took an honest look at my own self-sabotaging patterns and chose to no longer linger with the earthy smell of Mary Jane's medicine. We could no longer dance together daily because munchies are the inevitable consequence of one deep draw from her lips. If I continued playing with her fabulous fire, I would dissolve my desire to love the body I am building because I would grab a bag of candy and bowl of salty snacks without mindfulness. Then I would wake with a tummy ache and a head full of guilt.

Feeling my emotions allowed me to understand the roots of my own trauma. Learning to balance my energies helped me work through life's challenges and obstacles with determination, patience, ease and grace. Numbing was an avoidance behavior that distracted me from the beautiful opportunity to heal, sleep peaceful, wake restored and enjoy the beauty of my day.

Creating an evening self-care plan that included coloring, reading, watching movies and snuggling on the couch with Ralph helped me eliminate my need to escape. Dreams no longer haunt me to the same gut-wrenching degree. Night sweats, tears, and terror are no longer my normal. When the web of healing wraps me in her blanket, I allow the visions. I am able to see the truth in the tantalizing stories that meld past, present, future, and parallel lives. My reality became the peaceful reflection of my mind, and I felt safe in the world I had created.

Within the safety of my son's home, I could heal. The love Chance and Jessy shared with me was gentle. They allowed me to be sparkly, sassy, and quiet. Tears were shared as we continued to heal. The two precious gifts brought us love every day. Two-year-old hugs and kisses were valued as much as the four-year-old frenzy. Lennon James and Sunny Dawn Joy were the children whose value was immeasurable.

View my special message by scanning the code below
OR go to: https://qrco.de/AutumnFarewell

215

Chapter 40

Biggie Smalls

Chance and Jessy have a remarkable dog.
Biggie Smalls is a Boston Terrier whose determination and ambition are often too big for a dog who is so small. I admire him for so many of his troublesome traits.

When a bigger dog at the park comes too close to his family, he will protect them with all his might with his teeth barred growling his warning and attacking any dog who doesn't heed his warning. He will also chase down a ball without regard for the eighth commandment—though shall not steal. Biggie has not read the Bible or the dog park etiquette manual.

At home, he will destroy anything and do anything to get to his ball. The ball can be buried in the couch under a cushion beneath my granddaughter, Sunny, who is blocking the ball with her toys and blanket. Biggie will wait quietly while whining desperately, often, but not always, until Sunny either falls asleep or leaves the blanket fort that she has created. When perfect opportunity comes, Biggie will retrieve his ball.

When visitors come to Biggie's house, he will introduce them first to his ball and then to himself. Actually, no, that's not correct. He will say hello with his bark, jump two feet in the air, wag his chunky butt and race to get his ball. The goal is to have each visitor play fetch. He will pursue his purpose regardless of challenges. "Biggie no," will not deter him. "Biggie down," cannot dissuade. He will wait until his opponent throws the ball and then sprint to retrieve it. He will capture and chew it for a little while. If he lost his ball—and his mind—he would look for both until he found them.

I learned to be like Biggie. Every day I dig into the many opportunities that I have. I began the adventure in email marketing the day after Tania's court case. I was quite intrigued with the concept because I saw the limitless possibilities that on-line marketing offers.

I knew that my Tea and Tarot group needed a social media boost so that more people could learn how to have fun playing with tarot cards. I have been fascinated with tarot's mysticism since I was in my mid-twenties. Using tarot and oracle cards as divination tools has been fun way to help me journey through the experience of being a human. Email marketing was a powerful way to spread the opportunity and serve more people who are curious about seeking understanding and guidance with tarot cards.

I knew that I could chew through any obstacle just like Biggie chooses to destroy the base of the couch to get his ball if he happens to be left in a room alone and no one is there to rescue him. Biggie doesn't need to be rescued nor does he ask to be. This is one of the things, I admire about Biggie that I'm developing within myself. I do not need to be rescued, but, once in a while, I do allow others to help me.

For instance, my laptop stopped charging and Jessy offered to help me find a computer repair shop in Kelowna. I accepted her kind offer, crossed my fingers, prayed and hoped for good fortune. I trusted that nothing major was wrong with it so it won't cost much. Perhaps there would be no charge at all, or I would have the option to trade it in on a new model. I allowed the universe to help me on that one as well.

I needed to live my life with more effortless ease. For me, that meant allowing others to help me, and trusting that the Universe was supporting me. I was also increasingly aware of wanting to spend more time with Jarett. I wanted to visit him on Vancouver Island for the weekend of the anniversary of Emily's passing. I wanted him to show me around and I wanted to shower him with love. I didn't know exactly how it's all going to fall into place, and I knew that 360-degree planning wasn't necessary either.

Doubts, fears, limiting beliefs and other people's rules did not stop Biggie nor me. He followed his instinct and trusted without wavering. I was like him and fearless chased my desires because I knew that my determination would lead to fortune and success. I learned to work smarter not harder, used technology to my advantage, sought expert advice and collaborated with others.

View my special message by scanning the code below
OR go to: https://qrco.de/BiggieSmalls

Chapter 41

Many Feathers

I had to make a choice. Keep on running around and around and around, hold on tight while the wheel and the hamster spun with me, or be kind to myself. Sounded like an easy choice to a chooser who was easily a quitter. Instead of striving to meet my goals, I chose to connect with my higher self in the meadow where I could find peace.

Morning meditation allowed me to spend time in my sacred space. When I allowed enough time, I was able to visualize and connect with my spirit guide. He was a beautiful man with long jet-black hair, a fierce red and black headdress that held many feathers, a medicine bag and a drum.

Each time we met the feathers changed, and the medicines he offered were specific for the journey I was to take. He wore eagle feathers when he came to help me conquer fear and overcome adversity. Parrot feathers were adorned when he reminded me to be aware of what I was saying to myself and others. If I needed to come out from the shadows and shine, his head dress was decorated like the plume of a peacock.

The medicines he shared with me were powerful and specific for the malady that caused disorder or disease in my body, especially ones that were chronic or deep seated. He offered mugwort to encourage me to practice lucid dreaming. When it was important to feel and remember my dreams clearly upon waking, I brewed a lovely cup of mugwort, hibiscus and peppermint tea before bed.

Each beat on his drum deepened my connection to all creation. I learned how valuable the sacred sounds were during my meditation and prayer time. When I listened to his drumming, I felt the heartbeat of people, animals and Mother Earth herself.

My spirit guide met me in the meadow where the grass was high, and the river flowed into the ocean. I created this space because I felt safe there. He came and brought me to the fire where he taught me to pray to the Great Creator of One. He taught me the universal language of love which helped me bridge the gaps within cultures, beliefs, religions and traditions.

Each time I met with him, I would focus on my breath, and simply breathe. I allowed myself to be with him until the lesson was complete. I learned to stop racing for the finish line or be distracted by my list of many things. I enjoyed the simplicity of being and enjoyed each moment.

Many Feathers taught me to enjoy the blessing in each day, wear my own warrior head dress with pride, dance to the beat of my own drum and stay my course as a humble, peaceful warrior.

View my special message by scanning the code below
OR go to: https://qrco.de/ManyFeathers

Chapter 42

Transitory Greatness

The day before my fifty-fourth birthday, October 8, 2023, I woke from a dream at 5:03 to the words "transitory greatness." With pen and paper, I digested the message that my angels sent to me. During my dream, I astral traveled quickly between timelines. Different versions of my life were shown to me to help me understand my unique abilities as a healer, speaker, writer and leader. During this beautiful Out-of-Body Experience, OBE, I was able to jump between different time and space realities. It was an incredible experience where the laws of physics did not apply, and my thoughts and emotions influenced my surroundings.

Before I could write, I needed to reconnect to my physical body and consciousness, thinking mind. I rolled out of bed, placed my feet on the floor, took a deep breath and began repeating transitory greatness. I walked to the easy-chair in the living room, sat down, reached for my journal and pen. I wrote the two words down, closed the journal and placed my pen on the side table.

Then, I took the next crucial step and went into the kitchen to turn the coffee maker on. Java helped me transition from the sweet, gentle, easy, flowing energy of dream to the physical action of writing. I loved the smell of the brew and the sound the coffee maker made that mixed perfectly with the ticking clock. I emptied the dishwasher while the coffee brewed and focused on my breath. I was grateful for the opportunity to live another day.

I studied the beauty of each plate, bowl, cup, knife, fork and spoon. With gratitude I opened the cupboard doors and gave thanks for my beautiful life. I looked at the pictures on my walls and the plants that decorated our living room. I counted my blessings as I walked into the living room and stood before my sacred ritual altar.

I reached for my matches and lit one candle. I began reciting my morning prayer, "God, grant me the serenity to accept the things I cannot change." Acceptance is a key part of my recovery, and this part of the prayer asked for peace of mind and calmness to accept the limitations of life and the things that were beyond my control. It emphasized the importance of finding inner peace amidst external circumstances.

I struck another match and ignited the second candle, "God, grant me the courage to change the things I can." I prayed for the strength and bravery to take action where possible and necessary. This part of the prayer encouraged proactive behavior and the willingness to make changes in areas where I had control and influence. I knew a fundamental strategy for success was imperfect action instead of perfection because only God had the power to create perfection.

I sighed and lit the third candle, "God, grant me the wisdom to know the difference." I asked for assistance with discernment and understanding to differentiate between what can and cannot be changed. I knew how much I needed insight and clear thinking to navigate life's challenges effectively.

I used a fourth candle that reminded me of the importance of my faith. I sparked a match, lit the wick and began to pray to Archangel Micheal. I asked him to take care of my loved ones and to help me forgive those who had caused me harm.

I prayed for Jarett and Amanda who were struggling with their health. I prayed for Chance, Jessy, Sunny and Lennon who were working through bedtime routine challenges. I prayed for Amanda, Matt and their unborn child.

My fears always involved my children, and I asked my angels to help me trust that they were capable of making their own decisions. I asked Archangel Micheal to surround them with love, light, protection and peace.

Then I asked him to help me forgive those who had knowingly or unknowingly caused me harm. I watched the flame flicker as layers of anger, irritation, frustration and resentments dissolved from my body. Prayer helped me prepare for meditation because it allowed me to empty my mind of thoughts that didn't serve my greater good.

Then, I sat down on the couch and began focusing on my breathing. Conscious breath work allowed me to sink deeper into my body and focus on any areas of tension. I visualized a soft, white healing light penetrating the space between my eye brows where my third eye was located. Meditating on this chakra enhanced my ability to perceive the deeper truths of my existence.

I knew that all that needed to be done had already been done and yet my desire to create a better world for my children often overwhelmed me. The expectation to know all the right answers was exhausting and I often felt powerfulness to help them work through the challenges of life. Focusing in this area allowed me to see that there were many loving and supportive forces assisting us all. I was able to rest in knowing that all was well in my world.

My gratitude and meditation practice were integral parts of my sacred rituals because they helped me raise my vibrational energy. I also chose my coffee cup with care each morning ensuring that the message was inspiring, empowering, cheerful and colorful. I picked my clothes with careful consideration because the colors, fabrics, style and feel had the power to improve my wellbeing. The only dress code I followed was comfortable and fun with positive messaging.

Following a healthy, self-care practice became increasingly important to me as I developed my intuitive skills and psychic medium talents. I followed a simple strategy that focused on the four elements: Water, Fire, Air and Earth. Drinking plenty of water helped me stay hydrated. Epson salt baths with essential oils helped me release tension and relax. Lighting candles and smudging allowed me to connect with the power of fire. I practiced the four-candle ritual every morning and smudged with sage, sweetgrass, cedar, tobacco and palo santo throughout the day. Sitting outside on the ground allowed me to feel the breeze and connect with the earth.

View my special message by scanning the code below
OR go to: https://qrco.de/TransitoryGreatness

SCAN ME

Chapter 43

Out of My Comfort Zone

I turned fifty-four years old and reflected on
the life I had created with Ralph. I was happy, loved, content
and unwilling to live one more year regretting that we didn't
make our move toward more time spent in Mexico. Planning
vacations made us both happy because we had something to
look forward to. Each year we promised to spend more time in
Mexico, yet we never actualized our dream to spend more than
two months.

Watching my dad and Rita, sell their home and move to
Puerto Aventuras allowed me to see that being an expat was
possible. I wanted to experience the adventure of building a
new life with Ralph in the state of Jalisco where we could enjoy
the beautiful beaches, vibrant nightlife, rich cultural heritage
and adventure of building a new life together.

I knew that if I continued to stay in my comfortable life and
only vacation for a few weeks, I risked regretting not taking
the chance to live my dream of completely immersing myself
in the adventure of feeling fully alive. I accepted the fact that I
may fail miserably and regret leaving the safety of our home in
Alberta. Nevertheless, I told Ralph that I was willing to rent our
home out and travel in between Alberta and British Columbia
during the spring, summer and fall months. I no longer wanted
to feel stuck by the financial obligation of paying a mortgage.
I knew that we could manage a way of that allowed us to be
good caregivers for our parents, stay on our career paths, enjoy
our grandchildren and the warmer weather in British Columbia
while still retaining our multiple properties.

I was excited to become a tourist in Mexico for three months because I wanted learn the language, experience the culture, wake to the sound of the sea and walk the beach every day. I was excited to continue to create the Recover Your Joy program and never again need to depend on any company or organization to pay my way. Expanding my transformational breakthrough coaching to an on-line, virtual experience for both individuals and organizations allowed me to share my expertise in grief, trauma, recovery and transformation. I trusted that because I had already helped many, I would positively change the lives of many more.

I dedicated thirty minutes every morning to meditating, enjoyed a soulful shower with reiki, self-care love followed by an hour of writing and then twenty minutes to pivot and stretch my physical body. I knew that I needed to honour my body and listen to my doctor's orders to limit any strain on my upper body. I focused my actions on aligning with an organization that would allow me to share the joy of recovery, I knew that there was a way to follow my dream without sacrificing my physical body, mental wellness, emotional wellbeing and be enslaved to making ends meet for somebody else.

I began to actively seek soul connections with like-minded people who whose passions aligned with mine. My love of writing, guiding, creating, communication and family led me to actualizing my dream of sharing my message across the world.

My friend Elizabeth Jean Olivia Gagnon invited me to be a guest on her Talk show Miss Liz's Tea Making a Difference. Her desire to bring awareness to services that provide educational awareness about important mental health issues aligned with my passion for communication. She allowed me to share my experiences as a mother who lost a child, the Battered Woman's Syndrome, addiction and creating a life with more joy.

Our wonderful conversation led to an opportunity to be a panel guest with Adam Duval on the Mental Health Warriors. One podcasting opportunity led to another, and I met my Kick Ass Accountability coach Christopher Rausch. I learned to step into my own authentic, raw, honest and kind purpose and began hosting more guests on my own podcast platform Recover Your Joy. Each episode brought amazing guests with impactful messages for hope, healing, recovery and proof that healing was possible.

Manifesting my dreams into reality became really interesting when I began to play with the foundation of my safety. I focused less on who we would rent our house to, how much money we would charge, what we would do with the contents and more on the fun of creating freedom in my life. I pulled out my journal and wrote down what home meant to me and what was important for my new free lifestyle.

I wrote why having a home has always been very important to me. I began with the importance of quiet time and isolation at the end of the day. Heartfelt conversations often left me feeling empowered and then drained. Recharging at home was important. I love to cook because it helped me ground after connecting with spirit especially when I channelled. I imagined what I would feel like cooking in friendly homes with all the gadgets I needed. Sleeping in a comfy bed with the window open was a must for me too. I felt the bed, blanket pillows and the sound of nature. Morning coffee, meditation, an outdoor sitting area and the ocean or lake are what give my soul space to speak because I love to connect with nature. I imagined the taste of the coffee and the feeling of writing in my journal.

Then I shifted my focus to how Ralph would fit into my free life living equation. He was the much more conservative person in our relationship. He was the one who would never ever imagine owning a farm, a goat, a tractor, or a mountain cabin. He was the 360-degree planner who thought about the cost before the fun and the probable risk factors. I needed to factor in the possible hazards and remind him that we had an incredible success rate in all that we had already created together.

View my special message by scanning the code below
OR go to: https://qrco.de/OutOfMYComfortZone

Chapter 44

Nonna Sparkles

I will not dance with the devil. I will dance with delight, for I know beneath the shadow, there is always the light.

The day my third grandchild was born was full of magic. I was fully present to the complete experience because I knew the importance of creating a memory. Within the excitement of waiting to find out if my daughter-in-law Amanda birthed a boy or a girl, loomed the fear of the unknown. Fear was a dark thread weaved in the tapestry of my experience because memories of Emily's birth and death filled my mind.

I embraced each moment with two hands, two arms, a heart full of gratitude and curiosity. Living in the joy of special days while processing the deeply buried subconscious memories can create the FFF—Fight Flight Freeze—which kicks in when the desire to escape the big-bunny-dust-balls-of-yuck-fuck was palatable. For me, that meant I could taste tin which was a sure indication that I was gritty my teeth.

I knew that this was an opportunity to investigate, explore, integrate and bring into the light the unconscious, shadow parts of myself. I knew that my shadow consisted of aspects of my personality, behaviors, emotions, and traits that I repressed, denied, or felt ashamed of. I asked spirit to help me welcome my fears and insecurities and trust that they would be transmuted by their love and light. Transmutation is the process of transforming negative emotions, thoughts and behaviors into positive ones.

I immediately tuned into the tension within my physical body and relaxed my frozen jaw. Years of training in meditation allowed me to pinpoint the areas in my body that were holding tension. I began with the space between my eyes and traced the tension to my temples, down my jaw line and then to my teeth. Relaxing in the moment allowed me to control my fear which was linked to the memories of my own daughter's birth.

Transmutation allowed me to turn fear into courage, anger into motivation, and sadness into compassion. I accepted my negative traits and emotions without judgment. I also practiced self-compassion to remind myself that everyone has flaws.

Then, I was able to focus on the beautiful memory of Emily's birth which helped me visualize a positive birth for Amanda. I began to imagine all the wonderful birthdays that we would share as a family. I trusted that everything was well. Happiness was a great feeling and helped keep me stay calm and peaceful amidst the anxiety we all felt in the waiting room. I knew the importance of staying calm because it would help create a peaceful vibration for everyone. Focusing on my peace would help me and allow me to be a better support system for Ralph, his daughter Amanda, and her mother Brenda as well as the daddy-to-be Matt and his parents Mike and Tracey.

Worrisome feelings and anxious thoughts were part of the experience as well because fearful thoughts came from my memories of Emily's tragic death. I remembered that worrying doesn't take away troubles it takes away peace. I allowed the thoughts to come and go while focusing on my breath.

Each time Matt came down to the waiting area in the cafeteria basement we shared a sigh of relief. Three mothers and two fathers sat together in love and prayed for a healthy addition to our blended family. We held hands, prayed, hugged, cried and supported each other. Hours passed as day turned to night and still, we waited.

We took turns visiting Amanda in her room as she transitioned through the stages of labor. Each of us loved her and told her how wonderful she was and then told those who were waiting what had transpired.

When Matt came down to see us in a hospital gown to announce that they have a girl, I smiled. Ralph cheered, "I knew it!" and then turned to me with tears in his eyes and a huge smile. Matt assured us mom and baby were both well and then announced her name—Sara Emelia.

I allowed my tears to flow. I accepted that my tears were a mixture of joy and pain. I thanked all our angels for the love they had shared with us all.

View my special message by scanning the code below
OR go to: https://qrco.de/NonnaSparkles

Chapter 45

Tea Time

Vampire, honey-red, hibiscus tea soothes my root chakra, also known as Muladhara. The energy center located at the base of my spine was where my body contacts the earth when I am seated in the classic posture of meditation. I chose this tea to help ground my energies and withstand the challenges of today. I've purposefully mixed it with cinnamon to warm my body.

I chose Hibiscus today because I am uneasy about buying a fifth-wheel travel trailer. I worry that I am compromising my financial stability. What if I don't have enough money to pay my mortgage. I panicked about getting sick again with cancer. What if I got sick and couldn't care for my mother? I dwelled about being a good mother and daughter. Each sip of tea helped soothe my angst so that I could calmly look at my fear.

I began by dissecting the doubt of being able to support myself financially. I knew that my childhood and my relationships with money was at the root of my fear. I saw my mom struggle as a single parent. The damaging effects of her brain damage only allowed her the use of one arm. I watched her struggle to walk without falling and speak without stuttering. She managed to save enough money to buy us a home, pay for my college education, tithe at church and go on vacations. Her faith was strong and her determination admirable.

I learned to be strong because I mirrored my mother's tenacity. I stayed resilient through the challenges with my own health and finances. I ensured that my children were well cared for and saved money for their education. My strong faith helped me stay the course when life's challenges were great. Developing my skills as a healer helped me follow my calling as an accomplished energy worker.

I studied the benefits of teas like I have for everything that makes my heart go pitter-pat. I read books and research the ingredients of each tea I blend. Before I write the details in my website, I test each tea. How do I feel before and after I drink a cup? What differences do I notice in my mind and body?

I follow the try-before-you-buy strategy because I'm skeptical about believing everything I am told. I test drive different cars and listen to my intuition before deciding which vehicle to purchase. When I bought my gorgeous green SUV, I had a fabulous salesman whose knowledge was exceptional. His kindness, authenticity, determination, understanding and commitment helped me turn a difficult situation into a positive experience.

I told him that my silver Navigator needed to be traded in because Terry failed to make the payments. I had to choose between paying off the ten-thousand-dollar balance or trade-in and buy a new vehicle. When the salesman evaluated the condition of the vehicle, he discovered that it had been damaged in transit before it became mine. I was shocked to be told that the value was decreased significantly.

I focused on the lesson within the challenge. Anger would have led me to a frustrating experience, and I wanted to move forward to a happier feeling place. I was grateful that the salesman helped me get the best trade-in payout possible.

When I drove away in my brand new happy green ride, I felt a sense of freedom. I was no longer bound to the memory of another unkept promise. I focused on gratitude knowing that I had a new friend and transformed anger into joy.

View my special message by scanning the code below
OR go to: https://qrco.de/45_TeaTime

Chapter 46

Bye Bully

I picked up the phone to call Terry the day before his birthday. Helga wanted to know his mental state of mind. She was the voice of vengeance and justice who wanted to know when Nancy would get paid.

The phone did not ring. The number was not in service. I was grateful that I was unable to contact him. I knew better and yet the familiar desire for retribution rang one last time. The truth was that he doesn't have the money to pay me. The beauty was that I knew the universe would provide funding for all I needed.

I deleted the last number on my phone with his name next to it. I turned toward my future and my vow to never, ever try to contact him again.

I became more willing to forgive each person who had done me wrong. I woke in the morning ready to recover my peace. I wanted to dedicate more time to my *What Matters Most* podcast and invite guests who would show the world the beauty of recovery. I wanted rock stars, change makers, revolutionaries and legends to share their stories.

The next day, a friend in need called. I listened to her story. I heard her challenges and agreed to get together later in the afternoon.

We shared tea, had a deep soulful chat, laughed, cheered and made an agreement to meet more often. I wanted to hear more about how I could support my spectacular friend whose music inspired me. Her journey through recovery taught me that being raw and vulnerable was imperative to sustainable wellness.

I checked my heart and knew that I could shine light on the dark places causing her pain. I asked if she was willing to let me guide her toward an understanding about the connection between her physical and emotional dis-ease.

When she agreed, I explained how my family patterns affected me. I shared that my parents divorced when I was in elementary school and how I was able to maintain loving relationships with them both as I matured.

I began by explaining that my father taught me the importance of telling the truth. I explained how both of us overcame addiction and chose to follow our dreams. I shared my experience with endometriosis and cancer. I explained the emotional connection to my physical malaise.

Then I told her about my mother who insisted I study hard, go to church, be a good girl and finish what I started. When I decided to take creative writing courses in university, my mother loaned me the money because she knew I was struggling in my marriage, and she wanted to help me find a way to be happy. She asked me to promise to pay her back and to write the truth. I kept both promises.

I told her about my bonus mom, Rita, my stepmother, who helped me stay the course in my darkest days. Her stern tone, the one she used with my father, was seldom spoken to me. When it was, it was a softer, much more loving voice filled with care and respect. I called her often for guidance, courage, and honesty. I was both bold and soft because of her incredible influence on my life.

Our conversation shifted after my share. The dialogue changed to her story of trauma and resiliency. I listened and watched her live in the memories of times past.

I poured another cup of tea for both of us and listened until she emptied her mind of memories. Then, we talked about the future and our intentions. We agreed to say goodbye to the bullies in our lives who had caused us pain.

View my special message by scanning the code below OR go to: https://qrco.de/ByeBully

Chapter 47

One Last Wish

Spirit spoke to me often during meditation and sleep. Communication was easier when my mind was at rest. I started writing this chapter with two thoughts at 12:34 in the morning.

Each sweet thought floated in and out of my dreams like a chocolate-filled butterscotch candy. I fought to hold onto the vision and watched it fade away before I could gather the strength to find a pen and write down the details. Remembering the messages in my dreams was important because I know that Spirit was guiding me toward greater purpose here on earth.

The time I woke was a numerical angelic message of reassurance. The actions I have taken are leading me in the right direction. I was divinely guided, protected, safe and there was no reason to slow down or take a diversion.

I felt a soft peace within my body. I knew that clearing my mind of worry would help me dissolve the fear of forgetting. I knew that the possibility existed that my remembering could change to forgetfulness as I aged. I acknowledged the fear and asked my angels to help me heal my mind. I closed my eyes and allowed their love to penetrate through my entire body.

My angels showed me where the root fear came from by taking me back into my past. I saw my mom in a hospital bed and knew that the time was when I was ten years old. Seeing my mom after her brain surgery frightened me and left an imprint in my mind. I was afraid that I would be like my mom and have a speech disorder. The unhealed wound caused anxiety and panic. I allowed the fear to flow through and asked that Archangel Raphael to place his loving hands on my heart.

He helped me release the layers in my heart wall that caused my anxiety. I saw the champion in me who learned to overcome her speech impediment. When I was in grade two, I suffered with lisping. The gift within the challenge was that I became an exceptionally articulate speaker.

Archangel Jeremiel stepped forward wearing his clock of wisdom. He is the miracle worker who helps us undertake an inventory of our life so we can fix, remove or change anything that isn't serving us. Jeremiel is said to be the Archangel who gives us our heaven. His name means God's mercy. His message was for me to focus on how I can be of service. He shone a beautiful orange light around me and filled me with a remembering. Forgiveness is a natural part of who I am. I am free. I am merciful. I am blessed.

He showed me the baseball field where I first met Terry and invited me to return there to pick dandelions and remember that there was beauty in every weed. I needed to remember where it all began. I needed to see with my own eyes how beautiful it was. Learning to forgive was more than just talking about forgiveness. I must go to the place where we first met.

I drove to Archbishop O'Leary High School and saw that it had been renovated. The baseball diamond where I once played was old and weathered. The well-manicured grass had become a field of dandelions. I took off my shoes and walked barefoot to the center of the field. I closed my eyes, felt the warmth of the sun and connected with the warm light of love. When I opened my eyes, I saw one perfect dandelion with a soft, white blossom full of seed. I picked it, made a wish and blew the seeds into the field.

View my special message by scanning the code below
OR go to: https://qrco.de/OneLastWish

May my heart continue to heal,
and my life be filled with more joy.

About the Author

Nancy Nance is an internationally best-selling author, public speaker, intuitive breakthrough coach and psychic medium from Edmonton, Alberta, Canada. She is an energy healer whose strategies are brilliant, effective, supportive and filled with love.

Nancy's innovative methods help you breakthrough limitations, fear, doubt, anxiety, obstacles and challenges. Her breakthrough coaching program Recovery Your Joy is an opportunity for customized support. Her guidance will help you improve your emotional, physical, financial and spiritual wellness.

Nancy believes you are a gift and is here to offer you hope for a better way of being.

https://linktr.ee/exponentialjoy

I would love a review! Please post a review on Amazon or whichever platform you purchased the book.

Manufactured by Amazon.ca
Bolton, ON